W9-BGX-590

GETTING BY IN ITALIAN

Second Edition

A QUICK BEGINNER'S COURSE FOR TOURISTS AND BUSINESS PEOPLE

Emmanuela Tandello

In cooperation with BBC Languages

First edition for the United States
published 1996 by Barron's Educational Series, Inc.
in cooperation with BBC Languages
a division of BBC Worldwide Ltd.
Woodlands, 80 Wood Lane, London W12 OTT

A Word to the Reader:
Because exchange rates of foreign currencies against the U.S. dollar vary from day to day, the actual cost of a hotel room, a taxi ride, or a meal may be more or less than the amounts in this book. Please consult a newspaper, bank, or currency house for the most up-to-date exchange rate.

© Copyright 1992 by Emmanuela Tandello

Portions of the reference section of this book from *Italian at a Glance* by Mario Consantino.

All rights reserved.
No part of this book may be reproduced in any
form, by photostat, microfilm, xerography, or
any other means, or incorporated into any
information retrieval system, electronic or mechanical,
without the written permission of the copyright owner.

All inquiries should be addressed to:
Barron's Educational Series, Inc.
250 Wireless Boulevard
Hauppauge, New York 11788

Library of Congress Catalog Card No. 95-53095

International Standard Book No. 0-8120-8444-6 (book and cassette)
0-8120-9681-9 (book)

Library of Congress Cataloging-in-Publication Data
Tandello, Emmanuela.
Getting by in Italian : a quick beginner's course for tourists and business people / Emmanuela Tandello.
p. cm.
Rev. ed. of: Get by in Italian. c1992.
ISBN 0-8120-8444-6 (book-cassette pkg.). —ISBN 0-8120-9681-9 (book)
1. Italian language—Textbooks for foreign speakers—English.
I. Tandello, Emmanuela. Get by in Italian. II. Title.
PC1128.T36 1996
458.2'421—dc20 95-53095
CIP

Printed in Hong Kong
987654

CONTENTS

Map of Italy 4

Introduction 5

UNIT 1 Saying hello and ordering drinks 7

UNIT 2 Shopping 21

UNIT 3 Traveling around 36

UNIT 4 Getting somewhere to stay 51

UNIT 5 Eating out 65

UNIT 6 Meeting people and doing business 78

Reference Section 92

Key to Exercises 105

Word List 113

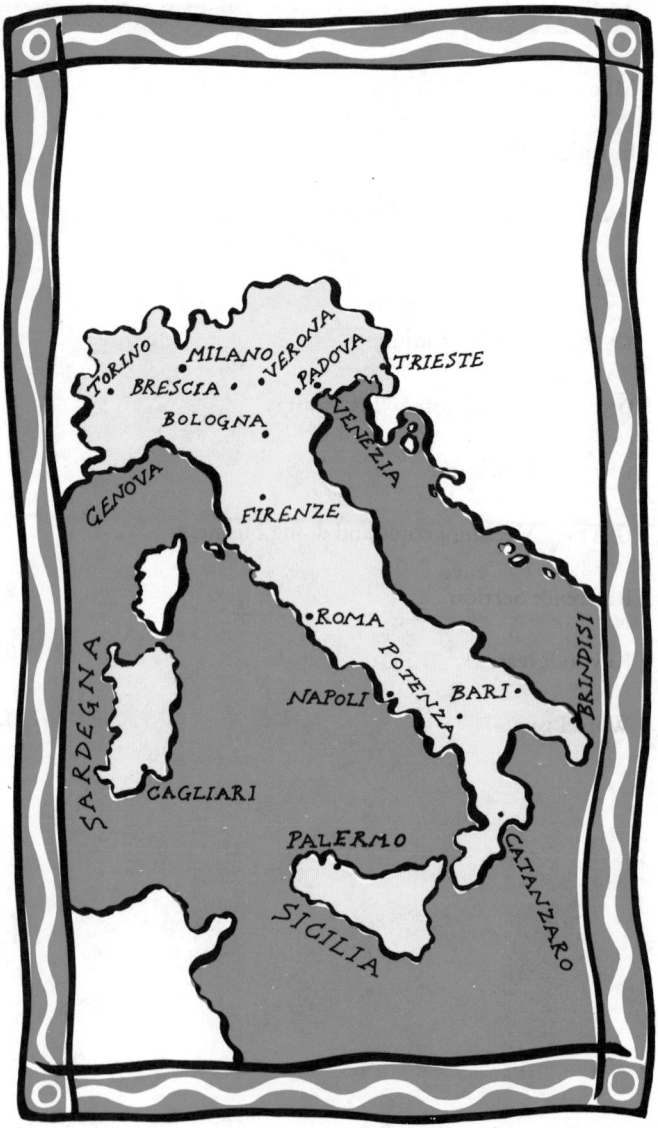
TORINO
MILANO
VERONA
PADOVA
TRIESTE
BRESCIA
BOLOGNA
VENEZIA
GENOVA
FIRENZE
ROMA
POTENZA
BRINDISI
SARDEGNA
NAPOLI
BARI
CAGLIARI
PALERMO
CATANZARO
SICILIA

INTRODUCTION

Barron's new *Getting by in Italian* is a six unit course for anyone planning a visit to Italy, whether for pleasure or business. It aims to provide the basic language and information for some of the most common situations of a visit abroad.

The course consists of a book and two 90 minute cassettes, to be used *together*. Each unit deals with specific areas of conversation: saying hello, shopping, travelling around, getting somewhere to stay, eating out, meeting people and doing business.

The *Getting by* book includes:

- the key words and phrases for each unit;
- the texts of the recorded dialogues in the order they'll be heard on the cassettes;
- notes on each dialogue and a section at the end of each unit giving explanations of the language met; you will need to refer forward to these explanations in order to do some of the exercises;
- background information worth knowing about Italy and Italian customs;
- self-checking exercises for you to do between dialogues, and at the end of each unit (*Can you get by?*).

  (When you come across the cassette only exercise symbol ☆, listen to your tape for your instructions *and* for your answer, as it will not always appear in the key).
- a short reference section or appendix containing a guide to the basics of Italian pronunciation and extra language notes;
- the keys to the exercises and the transcripts of the listening exercises that you'll hear on the cassettes;
- a word list.

The *Getting by* cassettes contain all the dialogues, help with the language used in them, and listening and speaking exercises. They give you plenty of opportunity to practice all the key words and phrases at your own pace. Words which are introduced on the tape can be found in the Explanations section of the same unit.

To make the most of the course:

- The book and cassettes are designed to be used together. But, of course, you can reinforce what you have learned by re-listening to the cassettes while driving, for example.
- The following symbols stand for book only ☐☐ and cassette only ☆ exercises.
- The cassette exercises and language practice have been devised to allow you as much room for repetition as possible. Pauses are left for you to repeat words and phrases and to give answers in the exercises; but winding back and listening again and repeating improves your mastery of the language – so do so as many times as you feel you want and need to! You will certainly need to listen to the dialogues several times over.
- The dialogues are authentic: they are recordings of real people using real language in real situations. There will be plenty of words you don't understand, just as there will be when you go to Italy. Don't panic! Listen for the words you do know, and try to understand the gist of what is being said from that. Equally, when it comes to speaking, don't worry about making mistakes; the important thing is to make yourself understood. Of course, if you've already learned some Latin, French or Spanish, don't hesitate to guess at the Italian forms; they are usually very similar.

We wish you good luck with your Italian . . . *Buon viaggio! . . . e buon divertimento!*

1 SAYING HELLO & ORDERING DRINKS

KEY WORDS AND PHRASES

buongiorno	hello, good morning
ciao	hello, hi, 'bye
buonasera	good evening
arrivederci	goodbye
grazie	thank you
prego	don't mention it
sì	yes
no	no
uno, due, tre	1, 2, 3
quattro, cinque	4, 5
sei, sette	6, 7
otto, nove, dieci	8, 9, 10
per favore	please
un caffè	a coffee
un bicchiere di vino	a glass of wine
quant'è?	how much is it?
posso cambiare . . . ?	can I change . . . ?

DIALOGUES

Listen to these exchanges on the cassettes:

SAYING HELLO AND GOODBYE

1

— Buongiorno.
— Buongiorno.
— Buongiorno.
— Buongiorno.
— Buongiorno.
— Buongiorno, signora.
— Buongiorno.
— Buongiorno.
— Buongiorno, signora.

buongiorno (literally good day) is used both to greet people and to say goodbye.
signora (literally madam) is more frequently used than its English equivalent.

2

— Buonasera!
— Buonasera!
— Buonasera!
— Buonasera!
— Buonasera, signori.
— Buonasera.
— Buonasera, dottore.

buonasera good evening, is the usual greeting from mid-afternoon onwards; it is used both to greet people and to say goodbye.
signori gentlemen; gentleman is *signore; signori,* however, is also used for ladies and gentlemen.
dottore doctor, though not necessarily a medical one; a title used for professional people such as engineers, solicitors, etc.

3

— Ciao!
— Ciao!
— Ciao!
— Ciao Isabella!
— Ciao!
— Ciao Sergio!
— Ciao Francesca!

ciao hello, hi! – the informal greeting used with friends and family. It also means goodbye.

4

— Arrivederci!
— Arrivederci!
— Arrivederci!
— Arrivederci!
— Arrivederci, buongiorno.

arrivederci goodbye, is used at any time of day, with anybody, and can be followed by *buongiorno* or *buonasera*.

SAYING THANK YOU AND DON'T MENTION IT

5

— Grazie.
— Grazie.
— Grazie.
— Grazie, buongiorno.
— Buongiorno, grazie.
— Grazie, buongiorno.
— Buongiorno, grazie, signora.

6

— Grazie.
— Prego.
— Grazie.
— Prego.
— Grazie.
— Prego.
— Grazie.
— Prego.

grazie thank you
prego don't mention it; please is *per favore*

LEARNING TO COUNT

7

— Uno, due, tre, quattro, cinque, sei, sette, otto, nove, dieci.

8

CATERINA Allora! Uno . . . di' uno . . . di' uno? Uno.

MARIA LUISA Uno.
CATERINA Due.
MARIA LUISA Due.
CATERINA Tre.
MARIA LUISA Tre.
CATERINA Quattro . . . Quattro, prova a dire.
MARIA LUISA Quattro.
CATERINA Cinque . . . Di' cinque.
MARIA LUISA Cinque.
CATERINA Sei . . . Di' sei.
MARIA LUISA Sei.
CATERINA Poi sette.
MARIA LUISA Sette.
CATERINA Otto . . . Sai dire otto?
MARIA LUISA Otto.
CATERINA Nove.
MARIA LUISA . . . e dieci.
ADULTI . . . Nove e dieci!

allora now then
prova a dire try to say
di' . . . say . . .
poi then
sai dire . . . ? can you say . . . ?
e and

Exercise 1 ☆
Listen to Sergio giving his daughter some practice at numbers. See if you can do the sums in Italian! Before you start, two new words: *più* plus, *meno* minus. The answers are in the Key on page 105.

Exercise 2 ☆
Listen to the cassette and try to write down the telephone numbers that are given.
(Transcript on page 105.)

9

FRANCESCA Puoi cambiarmi diecimila lire?

ISABELLA Sì certo. Mille, duemila, tremila, quattromila, cinquemila, seimila, settemila, ottomila, novemila, diecimila.

FRANCESCA Grazie mille.

ISABELLA Prego.

puoi cambiarmi . . . ? can you change . . . . for me?
certo certainly
grazie mille thanks (literally a thousand thanks)

10

SERGIO Vuole qualcosa da bere? Abbiamo limonata, aranciata, caffè, coca-cola, tè e acqua minerale.

vuole . . . ? would you like . . . ?
qualcosa da bere something to drink; you can adapt this phrase to other verbs:
qualcosa da mangiare something to eat
abbiamo we have
una limonata lemonade
un'aranciata orangeade
un caffè coffee
un tè tea
un'acqua minerale mineral water

ORDERING AND PAYING

11 A coffee

PAOLA Buongiorno.

CAMERIERE Buongiorno a lei.

PAOLA Un caffè, per favore.

CAMERIERE Un caffè . . . Pronti il caffè.

PAOLA Grazie. Quant'è?

CAMERIERE Novecento.

PAOLA Grazie.
CAMERIERE Grazie.

un cameriere a waiter; *una cameriera* a waitress
a lei to you; *buongiorno a lei* good day to you
pronti il caffè here is the coffee (*pronti* literally straight away, ready)
quant'è? how much is it?
novecento nine hundred

12 A cappuccino

PAOLA Un cappuccino, per favore.
CAMIRIERE Un cappuccino? . . . Ecco a lei il cappuccino.
PAOLA Grazie. Quant'è?
CAMERIERE Milledue.
PAOLA Ecco.
CAMERIERE Grazie.

un cappuccino espresso coffee with steamed, frothy milk
ecco a lei here you are; *ecco* here (it) is
milledue 1200; the complete form should be *milleduecento,* but prices are generally given in the shortened form

13 Tea, coffee and a cake

PAOLA Buongiorno.
CAMERIERE Buongiorno.
PAOLA Un tè al limone e un caffè lungo, per favore.
CAMERIERE Va bene. Un tè al limone e un caffè . . . Ecco a lei il tè al limone e il caffè lungo.
PAOLA Grazie. E una brioche e una pasta anche.
CAMERIERE Ecco a lei.
PAOLA Grazie.

un tè al limone a lemon tea; tea with milk is *un tè al latte*
un caffè lungo (literally a long coffee), a weaker espresso

va bene fine, OK
una brioche a bun
una pasta a cake
anche too, also

Exercise 3 ☆
You order drinks and snacks at a café.

14 A coke and a beer

PAOLA Buongiorno.
CAMERIERE Buongiorno.
PAOLA Una coca-cola e una birra, per favore.
CAMERIERE Una coca e una birra. La coca, la birra media o piccola?
PAOLA Piccola, per favore.
CAMERIERE Piccola . . . una birra piccola, pronti.
PAOLA Grazie, quant'è?
CAMERIERE Tremila.
PAOLA Ecco.
CAMERIERE Grazie.

una birra a beer
la birra piccola o media? a small or medium beer?

15 A glass of wine

PAOLA Buongiorno.
CAMERIERE Buongiorno, signora.
PAOLA Un bicchiere di vino bianco e un bicchiere di vino rosso.
CAMERIERE Va bene.

un bicchiere a glass; *un bicchiere di vino* a glass of wine; *un bicchiere di latte* a glass of milk
bianco white; *rosso* red; *un bicchiere di vino bianco* a glass of white wine. Two more useful words when dealing with wine are *secco* dry, and *dolce* sweet; *un bicchiere di vino bianco secco* a glass of dry white wine.

Exercise 4 ☆ ☐☐

Listen to the cassette. Michele asks for advice before ordering some glasses of wine. See if you can follow enough to fill in the following wine table:

VINO	BIANCO	ROSSO	DOLCE	SECCO
Brachetto				
Soave				

Exercise 5 ☆

You order some drinks in a café. Listen to your tape for instructions and answer.

EXPLANATIONS

SAYING HELLO AND GOODBYE

Buongiorno good day, and *buonasera* good evening, are used both to greet and to say goodbye to people.

Ciao is used for informal greetings; with friends, or family, but not with somebody you do not know well. Use the more formal greetings in all shops and public places, and when being introduced to somebody.

Arrivederci means goodbye, and is used at any time, with anybody. You can use it followed by *buongiorno,* or *buonasera; Arrivederci, buongiorno.*

NUMBERS

It is essential to learn them thoroughly; here they are again.

0 zero		
1 uno	100 cento	1000 mille
2 due	200 duecento	2000 duemila
3 tre	300 trecento	3000 tremila
4 quattro	400 quattrocento	4000 quattromila
5 cinque	500 cinquecento	5000 cinquemila
6 sei	600 seicento	6000 seimila
7 sette	700 settecento	7000 settemila
8 otto	800 ottocento	8000 ottomila
9 nove	900 novecento	9000 novemila
10 dieci		

You have also come across 11, *undici*.
1200 milleduecento; 2500 duemilacinquecento (sometimes in speech the *cento* is left out, so you will hear *milledue* and *duemilacinque* instead). More numbers appear on pages 44 and 94–5.

MASCULINE AND FEMININE

Words that represent people (e.g. man, woman, waiter), or objects (money, glass, etc.) are known as nouns.

In Italian, nouns are either masculine or feminine. Masculine nouns generally end in *-o (passaporto)* and feminine ones in *-a (birra)*; nouns ending in *-e (caffè, pensione)* are less predictable. This affects the articles ('the' and 'a') that accompany the words: in the dialogues you come across *un caffè* and *una pasta, un tè* and *una birra. Un* (masc.) and *una* and *un'* (fem.) are the three words for 'a'. Adjectives (words like 'good', 'old', 'green', 'fat', 'interesting', etc.) also change according to the gender of the noun: *un vino freddo* a cold wine; *una birra fredda* a cold beer.

WORTH KNOWING

CAFFÈ, BAR

Every Italian town possesses its own beloved old café or cafés, attractive, old-fashioned looking buildings which for centuries have been the center of the town's public life and gossip, and have witnessed its important cultural and political events. They may be more expensive than an ordinary bar, but are well worth visiting for a real taste of Italian life.

Bars are more recent institutions. Both bars and cafés sell alcoholic and non-alcoholic drinks, coffee, tea, and snacks, both sweet and savory.

Sometimes you will have to get the receipt (*lo scontrino*) at the cashier's before going to the bar and ordering. If you sit at a table *al tavolo,* you will get waiter service, *servizio al tavolo,* and may have to pay a lot more.

The *paninoteca* (sandwich bar) is a very recent development. The name comes from *panino* (roll) and it is frequented mostly by the very young, who gather outside rather than inside, to sip their cokes and eat the American-style hamburgers, or the many different kinds of *panini imbottiti* (filled rolls).

If you enjoy wine and would like to find out more about it, try an *enoteca,* a connoisseur wine cellar; here you can taste many different wines, especially local ones, bearing colorful and enticing names such as *fragolino* (strawberry-like), *dolcetto* (sweetish) and *vin santo* (holy wine).

DRINKS AND SNACKS

Coffee: *un caffè espresso* is a small cup of strong black coffee.
un caffè lungo is slightly weaker.
un cappuccino is an espresso with steamed, frothy milk.

un caffè corretto is a black coffee with a dash of either *grappa* or brandy.
un caffè macchiato is coffee with a dash of milk.

Tea: *un tè al latte* is tea with milk, but do ask for it *con latte freddo,* with cold milk, or you might be served boiled milk instead. Italians, however, prefer it *al limone,* with lemon, or, in the summer, they drink *tè freddo,* iced tea, served in a tall glass.

Chocolate: *una cioccolata calda,* hot chocolate, is generally served in the winter with whipped cream, *con panna.*

Sugar: *zucchero.*

Mineral water: *acqua minerale;* it can be either *naturale,* or *frizzante* (sparkling); you may also come across *gassata* for sparkling and *non gassata* for still.

Beer: Italian *birra* is generally lager-type, either brewed in Italy (*nazionale*) or a more expensive foreign brand (*estera*). It is always served cold.

Wine: *vino rosso* and *bianco.* Among the most famous white wines are Soave from Veneto, Tocai from Friuli and Verdicchio from Marche. Among the red ones are Barolo ('the King of wines') from Piedmont and Chianti from Tuscany.

Cakes: *una pasta* is the generic name for a small cake. In the morning it is customary to have *una brioche* with your *cappuccino;* this can contain *marmellata,* jam, or *crema,* custard cream, or it can be just plain, *normale.*

Snacks: *un salato,* or *salatino* (plural *salatini*) is an interesting change when you want a light bite: light pastry with cheese, spinach, anchovies or olives; a toasted sandwich is *un toast.*

Soft drinks: *aranciata* orangeade; *limonata* lemonade; *un frullato* a milkshake; *un succo di frutta* a fruit juice; *una spremuta* freshly squeezed fruit juice: *di limone* lemon; *di arancia* orange; *di pompelmo* grapefruit.

CAN YOU GET BY?

The exercises in this section will help you to check your progress. The answers to the exercises are on pages 105–112.

Exercise 1 ☐☐

WORD SEARCH. Can you find six expressions for greetings and thanks hidden in this puzzle? They are *buongiorno, buonasera, ciao, grazie, prego, per favore.* The puzzle works up and down, side to side, and backwards.

U E B S T E I Z A R G O M P

L N U A R P C C D F H A N Y

B U O N G I O R N O A L E S

L O N A D F E L P Q S U I T

O L A R T D D S O A F I L R

R I S T O P E R F A V O R E

Q P E A N R V O E B B C D I

A P R E G O I D Z Z F P N U

L A A E R I R D O Z P S V V

V L Z P D R R I A A E Q P Q

V U E E L O A I C R S V Z H

Exercise 2 ☆ ☐☐

Bingo! Listen to the cassette, where Anna will call the numbers. Cross them out on the card below as you hear them. You should be left with one number at the end.

1		700		7	
			900		
800		5		300	
	8		400		
600		10			1000

Exercise 3 ☆ ☐☐

Read the exercise first, then switch on your cassette. Give your answers aloud.

1 You want to order a glass of sweet red wine. Which will you say . . . ?

a Un bicchiere di vino bianco dolce
b Un bicchiere di vino rosso dolce
c Un bicchiere di vino rosso secco

2 Now you want to order a medium-sized coke and a small beer. Which will you say . . . ?

a Una coca piccola e una birra media
b Una coca media e una birra piccola
c Una coca media e una birra media

3 You want to order a coffee laced with *grappa*. Which will you ask for . . . ?

a un caffè macchiato
b un caffè lungo
c un caffè corretto

4 Now you want something to eat. Which will you say . . . ?

a una pasta
b un'aranciata
c una spremuta

5 If you ask *Quant'è?*, which answer would you expect to hear . . . ?

a Uno, sette, cinque, otto, zero, due
b duemila
c grazie mille

2 SHOPPING

KEY WORDS AND PHRASES

posso cambiare . . . ?	can I change . . . ?
un etto	100 grams
questo	this, this one
un pezzo di . . .	a piece of
basta (così)	that's enough
Ha . . . ?	Do you have . . . ?
quanto costa?	how much does it cost?
quanto costano?	how much do they cost?
troppo caro	too expensive
posso vederlo?	can I see it?

DIALOGUES

AT THE BANK

1 Changing a Eurocheque

FRANCESCA Buongiorno.
IMPIEGATA Buongiorno.
FRANCESCA Posso cambiare un Eurocheque?
IMPIEGATA Sì, certo. Al massimo di trecentomila lire.
FRANCESCA Benissimo.
IMPIEGATA Il suo documento?
FRANCESCA Ecco.

un'impiegata a female employee; *un impiegato* is a male employee
posso can I?, may I?; *cambiare* to change; *posso cambiare . . . ?* can I change . . . ?
certo certainly
al massimo di trecentomila lire to a maximum of 300,000 lira
il suo your, yours
documento (literally document) identification, usually a passport
lira, plural *lire,* is the Italian currency – see the *Worth Knowing* section in this unit

2 Changing a traveler's check

STEPHANIE	Posso cambiare questo traveler's check, per favore?
IMPIEGATA	Sì, certo. È di cento sterline?
STEPHANIE	Sì.
IMPIEGATA	Bene. Il suo passaporto?
STEPHANIE	Ecco.
IMPIEGATA	Può firmare il suo traveler's check?
STEPHANIE	Ecco.
IMPIEGATA	Bene. Si accomodi in cassa. Arrivederci.
STEPHANIE	Arrivederci. Grazie, signora.

è is
di cento sterline for a hundred pounds; *una sterlina* (pl. *sterline*) one pound sterling; *un dollaro* (pl. *dollari*) one dollar
bene good (literally well)
un passaporto passport
può? can you? will you please?
firmare to sign; *può firmare?* can you sign?
si accomodi in this situation is a polite way to direct you to *la cassa,* the cashier's counter, but it is also used to show somebody in, and to get him or her to sit down; please sit down, make yourself comfortable.

Exercise 1 ☆
See how well you can get by at the bank. You want to change a Eurocheque and 100 dollars.

BUYING FOOD

3 Peaches

PAOLA	Buongiorno.
FRUTTIVENDOLO	Buongiorno.
PAOLA	Quattro pesche, per favore.
FRUTTIVENDOLO	Va bene. Tremila.
PAOLA	Grazie, ecco a lei.

il fruttivendolo the fruitseller
pesche peaches (sing. *una pesca*)

4 Rolls

PAOLA	Buongiorno.
NEGOZIANTE	Buongiorno.
PAOLA	Quattro panini, per favore.
NEGOZIANTE	Sì, subito . . . vuole normali?
PAOLA	Sì, questi, per favore.
NEGOZIANTE	Basta così?
PAOLA	Basta così, grazie.
NEGOZIANTE	Sei e cinquanta.

un, una negoziante shopkeeper
un panino a roll
normale ordinary
vuole? would you like?
questi these
basta così it is enough, that's all

5 200 grams of ham

SALUMIERE	Buongiorno, signora.

MARGHERITA Buongiorno.
SALUMIERE Mi dica.
MARGHERITA Vorrei due etti di prosciutto.
SALUMIERE Cotto o crudo?
MARGHERITA Cotto. Questo.
SALUMIERE Va bene.
MARGHERITA Bene. Quant'è?
SALUMIERE Cinquemila e trecento lire.

il salumiere works in *una salumeria,* selling cooked meats and salami, and often groceries as well
mi dica may I help you?; you will also hear *desidera?* and *prego?*
vorrei I'd like; you can use this phrase with verbs, too: *vorrei bere,* I'd like to drink. Another phrase for ordering is: *mi dà . . . ?* will you give me . . . ?
un etto 100 grams
il prosciutto ham
cotto cooked; *crudo* raw (i.e., cured, like Parma ham)

6 Cheese

MARGHERITA Ha del formaggio?
SALUMIERE No, mi dispiace.
MARGHERITA Va bene, grazie.

7

GIULIA Buongiorno.
SALUMIERE Buongiorno.
GIULIA Vorrei un pezzo di parmigiano, per favore.
SALUMIERE Quanto?
GIULIA Un etto.
SALUMIERE Basta così?
GIULIA Sì, grazie.
SALUMIERE Dopo?
GIULIA Basta, grazie.
SALUMIERE Grazie a lei, molto gentile . . .

Ha . . . ? do you have?
del formaggio any/some cheese?
no, mi dispiace I am afraid not
un pezzo di parmigiano a piece of parmesan (this cheese is generally grated at home). If you want to say a little of, the expression is *un po' di*.
quanto? how much? *quanti?* how many?
dopo (literally) afterwards. Here are two other questions you will regularly be asked in shops; *altro?* anything else? *poi?* then?, next?
basta, grazie that's all, thanks
molto gentile very kind of you

Exercise 2 ☆
You are buying some ham, some cheese and some butter (*il burro*).

8 Ice cream

PAOLA	Buongiorno.
GELATAIO	Buongiorno, signorina.
PAOLA	Un gelato, per piacere.
GELATAIO	Un gelato, sì. Che gusto desidera?
PAOLA	(*pointing*) Eh, questo qui.
GELATAIO	Questo qui, eh, al limone?
PAOLA	Sì, grazie.
GELATAIO	Al limone. Pronti il gelato.
PAOLA	Quant'è?
GELATAIO	Mille.
PAOLA	Ecco.
GELATAIO	Grazie, arrivederci.
PAOLA	Buongiorno, grazie.

the *gelataio* works in *una gelateria* and sells *gelati* ice creams
signorina miss – now generally used with very young women
un gelato an ice cream

per piacere please (an alternative to *per favore*)
che gusto? what flavor?
desidera would you like
questo qui this one here

Exercise 3 ☆
Listen to another *gelataio* listing the flavors he sells. See if you can catch whether he sells peach-flavored ice cream and chocolate ice cream. (Transcript on page 107.)

AT THE PHARMACIST'S/CHEMIST'S

9

PAOLA	Buongiorno.
FARMACISTA	Buongiorno, signora.
PAOLA	Ha qualcosa per la diarrea?
FARMACISTA	Si, queste gocce. Quindici tre volte al giorno.
PAOLA	Benissimo. Quant'è?
FARMACISTA	Eh . . . sono seimilanovecentocinquanta lire.
PAOLA	Ecco a lei.
FARMACISTA	Grazie.

una farmacista pharmacist works in a *farmacia* pharmacy
qualcosa per something for; *ha qualcosa per la diarrea?* do you have anything for diarrhea?
gocce (sing., *goccia*) drops
quindici fifteen
volte times
al giorno per day; *tre volte al giorno* three times a day
benissimo very good (literally, very well)
sono seimilanovecentocinquanta lire it is 6,950 lire

AT THE TOBACCONIST'S

10 Buying *gettoni*

PAOLA Buongiorno.
NEGOZIANTE Buongiorno.
PAOLA Ha dei gettoni, per favore?
NEGOZIANTE Sì, certo, quanti?
PAOLA Uno.
NEGOZIANTE Eh, ecco, tenga.
PAOLA Quant'è?
NEGOZIANTE Eh, duecento.
PAOLA Ecco a lei.
NEGOZIANTE Grazie.
PAOLA Grazie, buongiorno.
NEGOZIANTE Buongiorno.

un gettone (pl. *gettoni*) a telephone token; *dei gettoni* some/any telephone tokens
ecco tenga here it is (literally here, take it)

11 Buying a phone card

PAOLA Buongiorno.
NEGOZIANTE Buongiorno.
PAOLA Ha delle carte telefoniche?
NEGOZIANTE Sì. Da cinquemila, o da diecimila lire?
PAOLA Una da cinquemila, per favore.
NEGOZIANTE Ecco.
PAOLA Grazie, buongiorno.
NEGOZIANTE Buongiorno, grazie.

carta telefonica (pl. *carte telefoniche*) a phone card; *delle carte telefoniche* some, any phone cards
da expresses value; *da cinquemila* a five thousand lire (phone card)

12 Buying stamps

TABACCAIO	Buongiorno. Prego?
GIULIA	Buongiorno. Quanto costano i francobolli per lettera per l'Inghilterra?
TABACCAIO	Settecento lire per lettera.
GIULIA	E cartolina?
TABACCAIO	Seicento.
GIULIA	Venti francobolli per lettera per l'Inghilterra.
TABACCAIO	Allora, dieci e . . . venti. Quattordicimila.
GIULIA	Quattordici . . . ho ventimila.
TABACCAIO	Ecco, seimila di resto.
GIULIA E TABACCAIO	Grazie.

il tabaccaio the tabacconist; he works in *una tabaccheria.*
quanto costano . . . ? how much do (the stamps) cost?
un francobollo (pl. *francobolli*) a stamp; they are sold per *lettera,* for letters, and *per cartolina,* for postcards
venti twenty
quattordici fourteen
Ho I have
(seimila) di resto (six thousand) change

Exercise 4 ☆
You buy telephone tokens, a phone card and stamps.

AT THE SHOPS

13 Buying a present

PAOLA	Buongiorno.
NEGOZIANTE	Buongiorno, signorina.
PAOLA	Quanto costa questo portafoglio?
NEGOZIANTE	Questo portafoglio costa ottantacinquemila lire.
PAOLA	Uhm . . . troppo caro. Ha qualcosa di . . . meno caro?

NEGOZIANTE Sì, ho questo sempre in pelle e costa trentacinquemila lire. Oppure qualcosina che costa venticinque.

PAOLA Posso vederlo?

NEGOZIANTE Certo.

PAOLA Va bene questo.

NEGOZIANTE Bene. Le faccio un pacchettino?

PAOLA No, grazie . . . Ecco venticinque.

NEGOZIANTE Benissimo. Grazie.

PAOLA Buongiorno, grazie.

NEGOZIANTE Arrivederci, buongiorno.

quanto costa questo portafoglio? how much does this wallet cost? You can also use *quanto costa?* on its own to mean how much does it cost?
ottantacinquemila 85,000
troppo too, too much
caro dear, expensive
qualcosa something; *qualcosa di meno caro* something less expensive; another useful expression is *qualcosa di più grande,* something bigger
sempre still
in pelle in leather
trentacinquemila 35,000
oppure or (else)
qualcosina (the diminutive form of *qualcosa*) a little something
venticinque twenty-five
posso vederlo? may I see it? *vederlo* is a compound word formed of *vedere* to see, and *lo* it
le for you
Le faccio un pacchettino? Shall I gift-wrap it? *faccio* comes from *fare* to do or to make
un pacchettino is a diminutive for *pacchetto* (package)

EXPLANATIONS

IL AND *LA*

il, l' and *lo* (masc.) and *la* and *l'* (fem.) are the Italian equivalents of 'the'. *il* is used with most masculine words: *il panino* the bread roll, *il telefono* the telephone. For masculine nouns beginning with *sc. . ., st. . ., sp. . ., ps. . .* and *z* use *lo: lo scontrino* the receipt, *lo zucchero* sugar.
la is used with most feminine words: *la pesca* the peach, *la carta* the card.
l' is used for both masculine and feminine nouns beginning with a vowel: *l'aranciata* or orangeade; *l'etto* 100 grams.
The plural of *il* is *i: i francobolli* the stamps; *i documenti* the documents. The plural of *lo* is *gli: gli scontrini* the receipts.
The plural or *la* is *le: le lettere* the letters; *le cartoline* the postcards.

DEL AND *DELLA*

del and *della* mean some, any: *Ha del formaggio?* Do you have any cheese? *della limonata?* any lemonade? *Ha della birra?* Do you have any beer?
The plural of *del* is *dei: Ha dei francobolli?* Do you have any stamps? *Ha dei gettoni?* Do you have any tokens?
The plural of *della* is *delle: delle lettere* some letters; *Ha delle carte telefoniche?* Do you have any phone cards?

PLURALS

You have come across the plurals of some nouns already: *lire, pesche, panini*. In general, the masculine plural ends in *-i: il panino, i panini*. The feminine plural usually ends in *-e: la cartolina, le cartoline*.
Some words, particularly foreign words used in Italian, do not change in the plural; *caffè* is one of them, and so is *bar: i caffè, i bar*.

QUESTO, QUESTA

questo, questa is the word for 'this' and, like other adjectives, it changes according to whether the word it refers to is masculine or feminine, singular or plural: *questo portafoglio* (masc.) this wallet; *questa pasta* (fem.) this cake; *questi panini* (masc. pl.) these bread rolls; *queste pesche* (fem. pl.) these peaches.

QUANTO COSTA? QUANTO COSTANO?

costare means to cost. *costa* is the singular form: *questo portafoglio costa ottantacinquemila lire* this wallet costs 85,000 lire; *costano* is the plural form: *queste pesche costano tremila al chilo* these peaches cost 3,000 lire per kilo.
quant'è? and *quanto costa?* are more or less interchangeable, like 'How much is it?' and 'How much does it cost?' in English.

DA

da expresses value: *una carta telefonica da cinquemila* a five thousand lire phone card; it is used with notes *banconote,* and coins *monete: una banconota da diecimila lire,* a ten thousand lire note; *una moneta da cinquecento lire* a five hundred lire coin.

WORTH KNOWING

BANKS

Banks in Italy are open from Monday to Friday, generally between 8:30 in the morning until 1:30 in the afternoon. To change currency look for the sign *Cambio.* If you wish to cash a traveler's check you will need to show your passport. The clerk will probably take a photocopy of the first two pages of your passport; this is common practice, and should not alarm you! There may also be a small charge (*il bollo*). You may also be asked where you are staying: *Dove abita?* You only need to reply with the name of your hotel.

Most Italian banks are equipped with express service counters working 24 hours a day, which accept most Visa cards. Other places where you can change money are the *Aziende di Promozione Turistica* (APT), to be found in all main railway stations, and at tourist information centers (*Informazioni Turistiche*); as well as at the *Uffici Cambio* (exchange offices). These have different opening times, so beware!

MONEY

The Italian currency is the *lira* (written £, like the pound sterling), plural *lire*. Banknotes (*banconote*) come in denominations of 1,000, 2,000, 5,000, 10,000, 20,000, 50,000, and 100,000 lire. The main coins are 50, 100, 200, 500, and 1,000 *lire*.

POSTAL SERVICES

The main post office in Italy is called *Poste e Telecomunicazioni*. The initials PT appear on the sign marking an individual post office, *ufficio postale*. *L'ufficio postale* is generally open between 8:15 A.M. and 1:30 P.M. from Mondays to Fridays; 8:15 A.M. and 12:20 P.M. on Saturdays. Mail boxes are generally red, and bear two different slots; *per la città,* for local mail, and *per tutte le altre destinazioni,* for all other destinations. There are different postal rates in Italy: *per lettera,* for letters, and *per cartolina,* for postcards. You can get stamps also from tobacco shops, easily recognizable by their distinctive sign: a large white T. Ask for *francobolli per Stati Uniti* when you are writing to someone in the USA. Because Italians tend to subsume the whole of the United Kingdom under *Inghilterra* (England) people generally ask for *francobolli per l'Inghilterra,* regardless of where in the UK they are sending letters.

SHOPS

la farmacia is the pharmacy. Pharmacies are open Monday through Friday. If you need a pharmacist during the weekend or at night, you will find the emergency number (headed *farmacie di turno*) on the door of most pharmacies. Here is a list of the most common ailments, and how to ask for something to cure them; *ha qualcosa per . . . ?*
il mal di testa headache
il mal di stomaco stomachache
il mal di denti toothache
il raffreddore a cold
For some ailments, instead of tablets (*compresse*) you will be given *gocce,* drops, to be taken at regular intervals.

alimentari local grocer's shop

panetteria baker's, sells bread, flour, cakes, and cookies

pasticceria pastry shop

mercato market

supermercato supermarket

frutta e verdura is the greengrocer's. Here is a list of produce you may want to buy:

mele apples
banane bananas
arance oranges
pere pears
pompelmi grapefruit
fragole strawberries
pomodori tomatoes
peperoni peppers
carote carrots
patate potatoes

You will probably want to buy these by the kilo or half-kilo: *un chilo, mezzo chilo.*

macelleria butcher's shop

cantina wine shop

profumeria the perfumery, also sells cosmetics

valigeria leather-goods shop; a handbag is *una borsetta* and a belt is *una cintura*.

TELEPHONES

In Italy you can telephone from a public phone (*telefono pubblico*), from a bar, or from a hotel. If you are calling from your hotel room, you may have to ask to be given the line: *mi dà la linea?* can you give me the line?
Public phones take *gettoni* tokens, and/or coins: 100, 200, and 500 lire. Many also take *una carta telefonica* a phone card. You can get these, too, from a tobacconist.
The code for international calls is 00, followed by the code of the country (44 for Britain, 1 for the United States), then the area or town code (without the 0), and then the telephone number of the person you wish to call. So, to call the US number 516-434-3311 from Italy, you would dial 00-1-516-434-3311.
Italian numbers, after the code (*il prefisso*) have between five and seven digits; generally each digit is said individually, but sometimes people will couple them: *cinquanta* (50), *venti* (20) *undici* (11); 0 is *zero*.
Phone calls can be local, national (*teleselezione nazionale*), or international (*teleselezione internazionale*); 113 is the emergency number for police, ambulance, fire service, etc.

CAN YOU GET BY?

Exercise 1 ☆
See whether you can memorize Anna's shopping list!

Exercise 2 ☆

Some practice at understanding prices. (Transcript on page 107.)

Exercise 3 ☆ ☐☐

Read the exercise, and then work through it with the tape.

1 You are buying a wallet. Which will you say?

a Vuole un portafoglio?
b Vorrei un portafoglio.
c Abbiamo un portafoglio.

2 You want to ask how much it costs. Will you say . . . ?

a Quanto costano?
b Quanto costa?
c Questo qui?

3 You want to ask if they have something less expensive. Which will you say . . . ?

a Ha qualcosa di meno grande?
b Ho ventimila.
c Ha qualcosa di meno caro?

4 You would like to see the cheaper wallet. Which will you say . . . ?

a Posso cambiare?
b Può firmare?
c Posso vederlo?

5 How will you say 'This one's fine'?

a Sì, certo. Quanti?
b Va bene questo.
c Cotto. Questo.

3 TRAVELING AROUND

KEY WORDS AND PHRASES

scusi?	excuse me?
dov'è?	where is?
ha una pianta della città?	do you have a map of the town?
per andare a . . . ?	the way to . . . ?
può ripetere?	can you repeat, please?
a destra	to the right
a sinistra	to the left
dritto	straight ahead
non ho capito	I have not understood
quale autobus?	which bus?
dove posso trovare i biglietti?	where can I get the tickets?
due biglietti per . . .	two tickets for . . .
un'andata	a one-way (ticket)
un'andata e ritorno	a round-trip ticket
prima classe	first class
seconda classe	second class
da che binario parte?	from which platform does it leave?
a che ora?	at what time?

DIALOGUES

ASKING THE WAY

1

GIULIA Mi scusi, dov'è la toilette?
ALBERGATRICE Al secondo piano.
GIULIA Grazie.
ALBERGATRICE Prego.

albergatrice hotelier (fem.)
mi scusi . . . ? excuse me . . . ? You can also simply say *scusi . . . ?*
dov'è . . . ? where is . . . ?
la toilette the toilet
al secondo piano on the second floor; on the first floor is *al primo piano*

2

FRANCESCA Buongiorno.
IMPIEGATA Buongiorno, signora.
FRANCESCA Ha una pianta della città, per favore?
IMPIEGATA Sì, eccola. Noi siamo qui in stazione; questo è il centro storico di Padova.
FRANCESCA Dov'è il Duomo?
IMPIEGATA È qui.
FRANCESCA Grazie mille.
IMPIEGATA Prego.

Ha una pianta della città? Do you have a street map of the city?
eccola here it is (*la* refers to *la pianta*)
noi siamo qui we are here; she is pointing at the map
in stazione at the station
il centro storico di Padova the historical center of Padua
il Duomo the cathedral

Exercise 1 ☆ ☐☐

Here are the names for some major cities. The presenter on the cassette will prompt you to ask for a map for some of them. For example: 'Do you have a street map of Padua?' is *Ha una pianta di Padova?*

Torino	Turin	*Venezia*	Venice
Milano	Milan	*Firenze*	Florence
Genova	Genoa	*Roma*	Rome
Padova	Padua	*Napoli*	Naples

See page 4 for a map of Italy.

3

FRANCESCA Scusi, dov'è la fiera?

IMPIEGATA Allora, fuori della stazione, a sinistra, sempre dritto; dopo il semaforo sempre dritto e subito a sinistra.

FRANCESCA Grazie mille.

IMPIEGATA Prego.

la fiera the trade fair
fuori della stazione outside the station
a sinistra on the left
sempre dritto straight ahead
dopo il semaforo after the traffic lights
subito a sinistra immediately left

4

STEPHANIE Scusi, per andare a Santa Giustina, per favore?

GIULIA Vada dritto, giri a sinistra, vada sempre dritto; dopo il semaforo, continui sempre dritto e sulla destra trova Santa Giustina.

per andare a Santa Giustina? to go to (the church of) Santa Giustina?
vada dritto go straight
giri a sinistra turn left
continui continue on
sulla destra on the right
trova you find

5

Listen to Stephanie on the cassette asking the way to Vicenza. See if you catch whether the sign indicating the direction for Vicenza will be on the left or on the right.

STEPHANIE	Scusi, per andare a Vicenza, per favore?
GIULIA	Vada sempre dritto, al primo semaforo giri a a destra e continui sempre dritto. A un certo punto troverà un cartello sulla sinistra che indicherà la direzione per Vicenza.
STEPHANIE	Può ripetere, per favore. Non ho capito.
GIULIA	Vada sempre dritto, al primo semaforo giri a destra, continui sempre dritto e troverà un cartello sulla sinistra che le indica la direzione per Vicenza.
STEPHANIE	Grazie mille.
GIULIA	Prego.

al primo semaforo at the first lights
a un certo punto at one point
troverà you will find
un cartello a road sign
che indicherà which will indicate
la direzione the direction
per Vicenza to Vicenza
può ripetere? can you repeat?
non ho capito I have not understood
che le indica that shows you

CATCHING A BUS

6

STEPHANIE	Quale autobus va alla stazione?
ISABELLA	Deve prendere l'autobus numero quattro.

quale autobus . . . ? which bus . . . ? *Quale autobus va alla stazione?* Which bus goes to the station?
Deve prendere l'autobus numero quattro. You must take the number 4 bus.

7

FRANCESCA Scusi, l'autobus per il centro, per favore?
IMPIEGATA Sì, allora, può prendere l'autobus numero tre, otto, o il diciotto.
FRANCESCA Eh, grazie. Ehm, dove posso trovare i biglietti?
IMPIEGATA I biglietti, fuori della stazione, subito a destra.
FRANCESCA Grazie mille.
IMPIEGATA Prego. Buongiorno.

l'autobus per il centro the bus for downtown
può prendere you can take
diciotto eighteen
dove posso trovare i biglietti? where can I get (literally find) the tickets? a ticket is *un biglietto*.

8

FRANCESCA Due biglietti per l'autobus, per favore.

BUYING A TRAIN TICKET

9

— Un'andata per Bologna.
— Un'andata per Milano, per favore.

un'andata a single/one-way (ticket)

10

— Due biglietti per Verona, andata e ritorno . . . e in prima classe. Grazie.

andata e ritorno round-trip (ticket)
in prima classe (in) first class

11

— Un biglietto di andata per Firenze, con supplemento rapido.

con supplemento rapido with supplement; *un rapido* is an Intercity train; you may have to catch one for part of your journey, in which case you must also purchase *un supplemento rapido*.

— Roma, andata e ritorno, con supplemento rapido Firenze-Roma.
— . . . Cassino, andata e ritorno, con supplemento rapido tra Pisa e Roma.

tra between

Exercise 2 ☐☐
How would you say:
a a one-way to Rome, please.
b two round-trip tickets to Naples, first class.
c Venice, round-trip, with a supplement for the *rapido* train.

ASKING WHICH PLATFORM

12

FRANCESCA	Da che binario parte il treno per Feltre?
IMPIEGATO	Treno per Feltre, binario nove. Treno diretto Calalzo.
FRANCESCA	Grazie.
IMPIEGATO	Prego.

da che binario parte il treno? from which platform does the train leave?
il treno per Feltre the train to Feltre (a little Venetian town north of Venice)
diretto a direct line—as used here—you do not have to change trains. *Diretto,* however, is also a type of train (see *Worth Knowing* section for this unit).
Calalzo is the final destination of the train.

AT WHAT TIME?

Exercise 3 ☆

Learn how to tell the time in the *Explanations* section, and then write down the times read out by Anna and Alberto on the tape. You may also need to refer to the *More numbers* list in the same section. (Transcript on page 108.)

13

There is no Dialogue 13 in this unit.

14

FRANCESCA A che ora parte il prossimo treno per Torino?
IMPIEGATO Per Torino diretto non c'è. Alle undici e venti c'è un treno per Milano con coincidenza.
FRANCESCA Ah, ho capito.

a che ora parte . . . ? at what time does . . . leave?
il prossimo treno per Torino the next train to Turin
c'è there is; *non c'è* there is not
alle undici e venti at 11:20
con coincidenza with a connection

15

FRANCESCA A che ora arriva a Torino?
IMPIEGATO L'arrivo è previsto a Milano alle tredici e quarantacinque, alle quattordici e dieci la coincidenza, a Torino alle quindici e cinquantasette.
FRANCESCA Grazie mille.
IMPIEGATO Prego.

a che ora arriva a . . . ? at what time does it arrive at . . . ?
l'arrivo è previsto per the arrival is scheduled for

Exercise 4 ☐☐ ☆

Listen to this exercise on the tape, and fill in the blanks in the timetable with the times of departure from Milano, the connection from Bologna and arrival in Firenze.

IL RITORNO DA **MILANO-BOLOGNA** PER **FIRENZE**

PARTENZA

											Exp					
Milano C.Le p	0:15											8:55	9:55	10:32		12:45
Bologna p	2:59	3:37	5:07	5:42	6:00	6:08	6:52	7:42	7:54			10:42	11:42	12:42	13:27	14:14

ARRIVO

Firenze SMN a		4:55	6:26	6:46	7:13		8:27	8:47	9:06			11:46	12:46	13:46	14:32	

BOOKING A SEAT

16

FRANCESCA Vorrei un biglietto per Roma in prima classe con prenotazione.
IMPIEGATO Va bene. Quando desidera partire?
FRANCESCA Giovedì.
IMPIEGATO Verso che ora?
FRANCESCA Verso mezzogiorno.
IMPIEGATO Abbiamo un rapido alle 12.59. Fumatori o non fumatori?
FRANCESCA Non fumatori, grazie.
IMPIEGATO Settantamila e seicento.

con prenotazione with a reservation
quando desidera partire? when would you like to leave?
giovedì on Thursday
verso che ora? at about what time?
mezzogiorno midday
fumatorio o non fumatori? smoking or nonsmoking?

17

Listen to the following announcement on the cassette; from which platform does the train for Bologna leave?

— È in partenza dal binario uno il treno diretto ventotto settantacinque delle ore dieci e cinquantasette per Terme Euganee, Monselice, Rovigo, Ferrara, Bologna/Parte dal binario uno il diretto ventotto settantacinque delle ore dieci e cinquantasette per Terme Euganee, Monselice, Rovigo, Ferrara, Bologna.

partenza departure; you will see the plural *partenze* on station departure boards
È in partenza il treno diretto ventotto settantacinque Stopping train number 2875 is on the point of departure
ore hours *delle ore dieci e cinquantasette* the 10:57 train
per for
Terme Euganee, Monselice, Rovigo and Ferrara are stations on the line between Padua and Bologna.

EXPLANATIONS

MORE NUMBERS

undici	11	sedici	16
dodici	12	diciassette	17
tredici	13	diciotto	18
quattordici	14	diciannove	19
quindici	15		
venti	20	venticinque	25
ventuno	21	ventisei	26
ventidue	22	ventisette	27
ventitré	23	ventotto	28
ventiquattro	24	ventinove	29
trenta	30	trentuno	31
quaranta	40	trentadue	32, etc.
cinquanta	50		

primo first
secondo second
Both take the same gender as the noun: *primo piano* first floor; *seconda classe* second class; *secondo piano* second floor.
More numbers appear on pages 15 and 94–95.

ASKING THE WAY, *DOV'È?*

scusi and *mi scusi* both mean excuse me and are used for apologizing, for addressing a stranger, and for asking people to repeat what they have said ('Sorry?'). However, 'Excuse me,' in the sense of 'May I come past please?,' is *Permesso.*

dov'è . . . ? where is . . . ?; *dov'è la Fiera?* where is the trade fair?; *dov'è la farmacia?* where is the pharmacy?

c'è, there is, can be either a question: *c'è una farmacia?* is there a pharmacy?, or a statement: *c'è un rapido alle 12:10.*

quale . . . ? which . . . ?; *quale autobus va alla stazione?* which bus goes to the station?; *quale treno va a Bologna?* which train goes to Bologna?

da quale . . . ? from which?; *da quale binario parte il treno?* which platform does the train leave from?

per for; *il treno per Bologna* the train to Bologna
da from; *il treno da Bologna* the train from Bologna

dritto straight ahead; *sempre dritto* is continue straight ahead for quite a distance (but is often misused as an equivalent of *dritto*); *sempre* means always.
a sinistra left; *a destra* right; *sulla destra* is on the right, *sulla sinistra* on the left.
la prima strada a destra the first road on the right, is often abbreviated to *la prima a destra* the first on the right.

al semaforo at the lights
fino al semaforo as far as the lights

dopo il semaforo after the lights
al, fino and *dopo* can be used with other nouns, too: *al museo* at the museum; *fino alla stazione* as far as the station; *dopo la farmacia* after the pharmacy.

di of; *la pianta di Padova* the street map of Padova; when you want to say 'of the town' though, you must say *della città.*

IF YOU DON'T UNDERSTAND

scusi, può ripetere? excuse me, can you repeat that?
non ho capito I didn't understand
ho capito (lit., I understood) understand

TELLING THE TIME

Che ore sono? What time is it? All hours (*le ore*) are feminine and plural: *le due, le tre, le quattro,* etc except for *l'una* one o'clock. So, *sono le due* it is two o'clock; *sono le tre* it is three o'clock; *sono le quattro* it is four o'clock, but *è l'una* it is one o'clock.

È mezzogiorno (masc.) it is midday, noon
È mezzanotte (fem.) it is midnight
a mezzanotte at midnight
da mezzanotte from midnight
fino a mezzanotte until midnight

Officially, Italian time works on the basis of the 24 hour clock. Minutes are added to the hour: *le tre e venti* twenty past three; or subtracted: twenty to three is *le tre meno venti*
23.35 *le ventitré e trentacinque*
8.15 *le otto e quindici*
7.45 *le otto meno un quarto*
The expressions *un quarto* a quarter, and *mezzo/mezza* express the quarter hour and the half hour: *le dieci e un quarto* a quarter past ten; *le dieci e mezza* half past ten

mattina morning
pomeriggio afternoon
sera evening
notte night
oggi today
ieri yesterday
domani tomorrow
stamattina this morning
oggi pomeriggio this afternoon
questa sera this evening
dopo pranzo after lunch

WORTH KNOWING

GETTING AROUND

BY BUS

Un biglietto turistico is a tourist ticket that gives you unlimited access to all buses for 24 hours. It can be purchased from railway stations, tourist information centers, and tobacconists'. Prices vary from city to city.

Whether you need an ordinary ticket, or a tourist one, you must purchase it before getting onto the bus.

la fermata is the bus stop; when at the bus terminal, generally found outside railway stations, look for the word *corsia.*

BY TRAIN

There are three main categories of train:
locale (a stopping train)
diretto (a slightly faster train; stopping at most stations)
rapido (express train); the last can be an Intercity train (abbreviated IC), or a Eurocity train (abbreviated EC). For both you need to pay a supplement, *un supplemento;* for the EC, this cannot be below a certain sum. In some cases, you must also make a reservation in advance; some IC and EC trains also carry first class only. Check these details in the timetable, *l'orario.* Look for the words *partenze*

(departures) and *arrivi* (arrivals). Also, look for the abbreviation RTD on the departures board; it stands for *ritardo* delay. If your train is late, the delay time will appear on the board.
You get your ticket from the *biglietteria* the ticket office.

BY BICYCLE

Noleggio biciclette In many Italian towns and cities you can obtain a bicycle to get around downtown, free of charge. The service is in fact provided by the local council, *il Comune.* You only need your passport (or any other document proving your identity). Look for the sign *Noleggio biciclette* at the railway station, or ask at the information center. There may be several hiring points in the center of town too.
Two major offices will give you all the information you need about the city or town you are visiting: the *APT* offices (*Azienda di Promozione Turistica*), and the *IAT* offices (*Uffici di Informazione ed Assistenza Turistica*). The latter are to be found in all railway stations.

One last useful expression: *Buon viaggio!* Bon voyage!

CAN YOU GET BY?

Exercise 1 ☆
Listen to the recording of the switchboard operator giving you the opening times of an office. Between what times is it open in the afternoon? (Transcript on page 108.)

Exercise 2 ☐☐
Buying tickets for buses and trains

1 You want to buy a bus ticket for downtown. Which will you say?

a Due biglietti, per favore
b Un biglietto, per favore
c L'autobus per il centro, per favore?

2 You want to ask which stop the bus leaves from. Which will you say?

a Da che binario parte?
b Dov'è il centro storico?
c Da che fermata parte?

3 You want to buy a second class, round-trip train ticket to Milan. Which will you say?

a Un'andata in seconda classe per Milano.
b Un biglietto di andate e ritorno, seconda classe, per Milano.
c Uno per Milano, per favore.

4 You want to leave today, at about two o'clock. Which will you say?

a Oggi, verso mezzogiorno.
b Domani, verso le due.
c Oggi, verso le due.

Exercise 3 ☆ ☐☐

Complete the following dialogue.

YOU	A one-way to Palermo in first class with a reservation.
IMPIEGATO	Quando desidera partire?
YOU	Tomorrow around midday.
IMPIEGATO	C'è un treno alle dodici e dieci.
YOU	Is there a supplement?
IMPIEGATO	Sì. Fumatori o non fumatori?
YOU	Non smoking, please.
IMPIEGATO	Va bene.
YOU	From which platform does the train leave?
IMPIEGATO	Dal binario numero tre.

Exercise 4 ☆ ☐☐

Using the map, follow the three sets of directions given on the cassette, and see if you can work out where they are sending you each time.

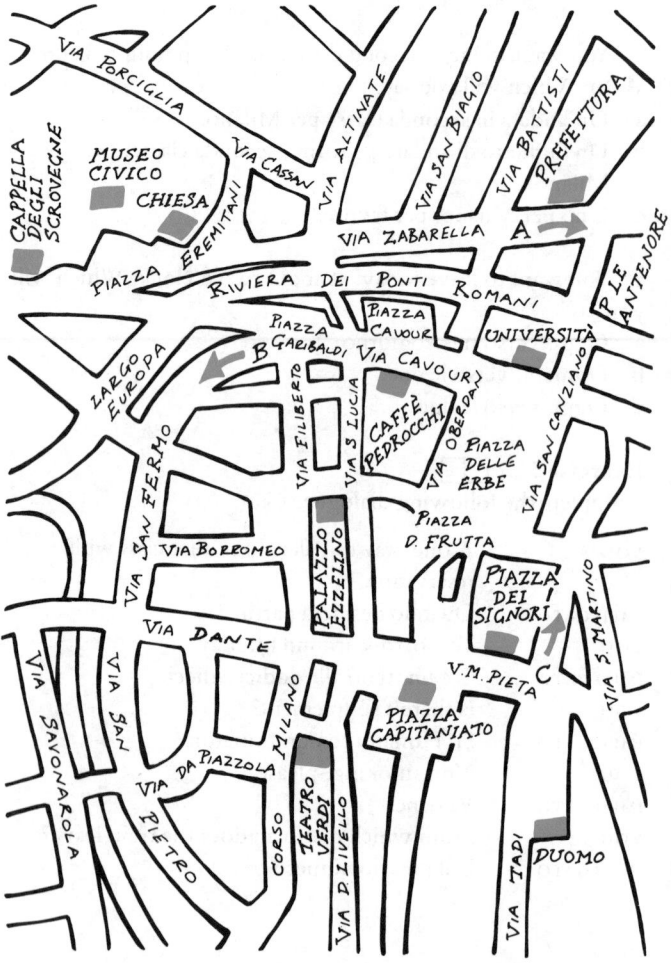

4 GETTING SOMEWHERE TO STAY

KEY WORDS AND PHRASES

ha una camera libera?	do you have a room free?
una camera singola	a single room
una camera doppia	a double room
una camera matrimoniale	a room with a double bed
una camera a due letti	a twin-bedded room
con bagno	with bathroom
senza bagno	without bathroom
con doccia	with shower
la colazione	breakfast
la chiave	the key
ho prenotato	I have booked
c'è anche un ristorante?	is there a restaurant, too?
un ostello della gioventù	youth hostel
avete posto?	do you have any room?
siamo . . .	we are . . .
un campeggio	campsite
c'è posto?	is there any room?
è all'ombra?	is it in the shade?

DIALOGUES

CHECKING INTO A HOTEL

A double room with bathroom

1

SERGIO Buonasera.
ALBERGATRICE Buonasera.
SERGIO Ha una camera libera?
ALBERGATRICE Eh . . . sì. Che tipo di camera?
SERGIO Vorrei una matrimoniale con bagno.
ALBERGATRICE Sì, va bene . . .

ha una camera libera? do you have a room free? The other word for room you will come across is *una stanza*.
che tipo di camera? What type of room?
una matrimoniale con bagno a double room with bathroom; *senza bagno* is without bathroom.

2

ALBERGATRICE . . . per questa notte?
SERGIO Sì. Quanto viene?
ALBERGATRICE Il prezzo è centoeottomila lire, esclusa la colazione.
SERGIO Benissimo.
ALBERGATRICE Posso avere il suo documento?
SERGIO Eccoli qua.
ALBERGATRICE Eh . . . Grazie. Questa è la chiave della camera, la numero undici al primo piano.
SERGIO Benissimo. Grazie.

per questa notte? for tonight?
quanto viene? (literally how much does it come out at?) is interchangeable with *quant'è?*
il prezzo the price
centoeottomila 108,000

esclusa la colazione breakfast excluded; breakfast included is *inclusa la colazione*
posso avere il suo documento? may I have your document?
eccoli qua here they are (referring to the documents, e.g. passports or identity cards)
la chiave the key
la numero undici number 11 (*la* refers to *la camera*)

A single room with shower

3

GIULIA Buongiorno.
ALBERGATRICE Buongiorno.
GIULIA Ho prenotato una camera.
ALBERGATRICE Sì. Il suo nome, per cortesia?
GIULIA Puchetti.
ALBERGATRICE Sì, la Signora Puchetti, è una camera singola con la doccia, per due notti.
GIULIA Sì.
ALBERGATRICE Giusto?
GIULIA Sì.
ALBERGATRICE Bene, allora, mi può lasciare il documento?
GIULIA Eccolo qui.
ALBERGATRICE Eh . . . Le dò la chiave, la camera è la numero trentatré al terzo piano. Si può accomodare.
GIULIA Grazie.
ALBERGATRICE Prego.

ho prenotato I have booked, reserved
il suo nome your name
per cortesia please, equivalent of *per favore*
una camera singola a single room
con la doccia with a shower
per due notti for two nights
giusto? is that right?
mi può lasciare il documento? can you leave me your identity

card (literally document)?
le dò la chiave I'll give you the key
al terzo piano on the third floor
si può accomodare is interchangeable with *si accomodi* please make yourself at home.

Exercise 1 ☆ ☐☐
You are checking into a hotel; complete the dialogue on the tape. Here are the details of your reservation:

NOME	SINGOLA	MATRIMON. CON BAGNO	MATRIMON. CON DOCCIA	NUMERO NOTTI
Martini			1	3

4

GIULIA A che ora è la colazione?
ALBERGATRICE Dalle sette e mezza alle dieci e mezza.
GIULIA E . . . c'è anche un ristorante?
ALBERGATRICE No, non abbiamo il ristorante, però posso consigliarle un ristorante qui vicino molto buono.

la colazione breakfast; lunch is *il pranzo,* and dinner *la cena*
dalle sette e mezza alle dieci e mezza from half past seven to half past ten. From is *da,* and to is *a* but as times are always *le,* e.g. *le sette, le dieci,* you say *dalle* and *alle.*
c'è anche un ristorante? is there also a restaurant?
però but
posso consigliarle I can recommend to you
qui vicino near here

Exercise 2 ☆ ☐☐
C'è anche . . . ? The presenter on the tape will prompt you to ask this question using some of the following words and

expressions for hotel facilities. For example: *C'è anch terrazza?* Is there also a balcony?

l'ascensore the elevator
la televisione the television
una vasca da bagno a bathtub
la piscina the swimming pool
l'aria condizionata air conditioning
la presa di corrente electrical socket/power point
il telefono the telephone
una terrazza a balcony
il servizio in camera room service
i servizi services, i.e. a toilet and a washbasin

MAKING A RESERVATION BY PHONE

5 (on the telephone)

ALBERGATRICE Leon Bianco, buongiorno.
SERGIO Buongiorno. Vorrei prenotare una camera.
ALBERGATRICE Sì, per quando?
SERGIO Per il 2 giugno.
ALBERGATRICE Un attimo in linea, per cortesia . . . Il 2 giugno, eh, siamo al completo, mi dispiace.
SERGIO Ho capito, grazie.
ALBERGATRICE Prego, buongiorno.
SERGIO Buongiorno.

Leon Bianco is the name of a famous hotel in Padua.
vorrei prenotare I would like to reserve
per quando? for when?
il 2 giugno June 2nd
un attimo in linea hold the line for one moment
siamo al completo we're fully booked

6

SERGIO Buongiorno.

ALBERGATRICE Buongiorno.
SERGIO Io vorrei prenotare una camera doppia.
ALBERGATRICE Sì. Per quando?
SERGIO Per dopodomani.
ALBERGATRICE Per dopodomani, dopodomani il 27 di maggio . . . eh . . . sì, posso prenotare una camera doppia. A due letti o matrioniale?
SERGIO Eh, matrimoniale, grazie.
ALBERGATRICE Sì, d'accordo. Soltanto per una notte?
SERGIO Per due notti.
ALBERGATRICE Per due notti. E quindi, domenica 27 e lunedì 28 maggio, partenza martedì 29.
SERGIO Certo.

io I
per dopodomani for the day after tomorrow; tomorrow is *domani*
posso I can
a due letti with two beds
d'accordo OK, (literally agreed)
soltanto only
per una notte for one night
quindi then, therefore
domenica 27 Sunday 27th
lunedì 28 Monday 28th
maggio May
martedì 29 Tuesday 29th
For the remaining days of the week and months of the year, see the *Explanations* section for this unit.

Exercise 3 ☆
Listen to the recording on the cassette. How much would you pay for a twin room with a shower and breakfast for two? (Transcript on page 109.)

CHECKING INTO A YOUTH HOSTEL

7

STEPHANIE Scusi, per andare all'ostello della gioventù, per favore?

GIULIA Vada dritto, la prima strada a destra, la prima porta a sinistra, e là c'è l'ostello della gioventù.

l'ostello della gioventù the youth hostel
la prima porta the first door
là there, (literally in that place)

8

GIULIA Buongiorno.

IMPIEGATO Buongiorno.

GIULIA Avete posto per questa notte?

IMPIEGATO Sì, in quanti siete?

GIULIA Siamo due ragazze e un ragazzo.

IMPIEGATO Bene, allora mi servono i vostri passaporti.

GIULIA Sì . . . tenga.

IMPIEGATO Grazie.

GIULIA C'è anche il ristorante?

IMPIEGATO Sì. Il servizio ristorante incomincia alle otto di sera fino alle dieci.

avete posto per questa notte? do you have (any) space for tonight?
in quanti siete? how many of you are there?
siamo due ragazze e un ragazzo we are two girls and one boy; *ragazzo* and *ragazza* are used for young people up to the age of 20.
mi servono i vostri passaporti I need your passports (literally your passports are useful to me)
il servizio ristorante the restaurant service
incomincia begins, starts
alle otto di sera at 8 o'clock in the evening
fino until

Exercise 4 ☆ ☐☐

Some reservations are being made at a youth hostel. Fill in the register page below specifying how many *ragazze* and how many *ragazzi* are booking in each time. Note that the page bears four different times, coinciding with each reservation. (Transcript on page 109.)

26 MAGGIO	RAGAZZI	RAGAZZE

CHECKING INTO A CAMPSITE

9

MICHELE Buongiorno.

CUSTODE Buongiorno.

MICHELE C'è posto?

CUSTODE Sì, certo.

MICHELE Allora, siamo cinque persone: due adulti e tre bambini, con una roulotte ed una tenda.

CUSTODE Ho il posto che fa al caso vostro.

MICHELE È all'ombra?

CUSTODE Sì, certo.

MICHELE Molto bene. Eh . . . quanto costa? per quindici giorni?

CUSTODE Quindici giorni ha detto . . . duecento-cinquantamila lire.

MICHELE Va bene. Allora lo prendo. Ecco i miei documenti.

CUSTODE Va bene. Glieli dò domani.

MICHELE Grazie.

c'è posto? is there (any) room?
siamo cinque persone there are five of us (literally we are five people)
adulti adults (sing. *un adulto*)
tre bambini three children (sing. *un bambino*)
una roulotte a caravan
una tenda a tent
Ho il posto che fa al caso vostro I have the space which suits your requirements
È all'ombra? Is it in the shade?
ha detto you said
lo prendo I'll take it
i miei documenti my documents
glieli dò domani I'll give them back to you tomorrow.

Exercise 5 ☆
You make a reservation at a campsite. Listen to your tape for instructions and answer.

Exercise 6 ☆ □□
On the cassette, Anna tells you where she will be working next year. Fill in the time-planner in the book with the English place-names. (Transcript on page 109.)

DIARIO	
GENNAIO	LUGLIO
FEBBRAIO	AGOSTO
MARZO	SETTEMBRE
APRILE	OTTOBRE
MAGGIO	NOVEMBRE
GIUGNO	DICEMBRE

EXPLANATIONS

DATES

Dates are always masculine in Italian. The first of any month is *il primo . . . : il primo giugno* June 1; after that, dates are not second, third, fourth, but two, three, etc: *il due giugno, il tre giugno;* you will also hear *il due di giugno, il tre di giugno,* etc.

DAYS OF THE WEEK

I giorni della settimana The days of the week

lunedì	Monday	*venerdì*	Friday
martedì	Tuesday	*sabato*	Saturday
mercoledì	Wednesday	*domenica*	Sunday
giovedì	Thursday		

MONTHS OF THE YEAR

I mesi dell'anno The months of the year

gennaio	January	*luglio*	July
febbraio	February	*agosto*	August
marzo	March	*settembre*	September
aprile	April	*ottobre*	October
maggio	May	*novembre*	November
giugno	June	*dicembre*	December

SEASONS

Le stagioni The seasons

primavera	spring	*autunno*	autumn
estate	summer	*inverno*	winter

orario estivo summer timetable
orario invernale winter timetable

aperto open
chiuso closed
chiuso per ferie closed for holidays
chiuso per turno weekly closing (day)
chiuso per lutto closed for mourning

QUANTO?

quanto? how much? takes the gender and number of the words it accompanies: *per quanto?* for how long? *per quante notti?* for how many nights? *per quanti giorni?* for how many days?

PER

per indicates duration: *per due notti* for two nights; *per tre giorni* for three days; *per un'ora* for one hour; *per sei mesi* for six months; *per questa notte* for tonight; *per domani* for tomorrow; *per il ventotto di maggio* for May 28; *per quando?* for when?; *per* is also used with quantities: *per due persone* for two people

DA . . . A

da . . . a from . . . to: *da lunedì a venerdì* from Monday to Friday; *aperto dal lunedì al venerdì* open from Monday to Friday (every week).
dal . . . al are used with dates, which are masculine: *dal due al tre di settembre* from the second to the third of September; *dal ventuno di luglio al sei agosto* from the twenty-first of July to the sixth of August.

IN QUANTI SIETE?

in quanti siete? how many are you? (2nd person plural form)
siamo we are: *siamo tre ragazzi* we are three boys; *siamo in tre* there are three of us, (literally we are three)

un ragazzo (pl. *ragazzi*) a boy
una ragazza (pl. *ragazze*) a girl
un bambino child (masc.)
una bambina child (fem.)
bambini children
un adulto (pl. *adulti*) an adult
una persona (pl. *persone*) a person

HA . . . ?

ha? do you have? *ha una camera?* do you have a room?
avete? do you (plural) have?
ce'è . . . ? is there?; *ci sono . . . ?* are there?; *c'è posto?* is there any room?; *ci sono bambini?* are there any children?
c'è is also used in statements: *c'è posto per oggi* there is room (for) today

CON, SENZA

con with: *con doccia* with a shower
senza without: *senza bagno* without a bath

WORTH KNOWING

GETTING A HOTEL ROOM

If you haven't booked in advance, you can get advice from the ATP and IAT offices already mentioned in the previous chapter.

pensione completa full board
mezza pensione half board
colazione breakfast
colazione inclusa breakfast included
colazione esclusa breakfast excluded

pranzo is the main meal of the day, generally consumed at lunch time
cena is the evening meal and can either be a formal meal or just supper

Hotels are now generally classified according to the international star code, but you still find them classified in first, second and third category: *di prima, seconda e terza categoria*.

Pensioni offer more modest accommodation.

Ostelli della gioventù youth hostels have greatly developed in Italy over the past ten years. Every major town has one. They are well-run, cheap and pleasant.

Tourist attractions: museums and art galleries are generally closed on Mondays; for some monuments, however, as well as major exhibitions, you must book your visit in advance. APT offices will generally be able to help you with the bookings.

CAN YOU GET BY?

Exercise 1 ☐☐ ☆
"Thirty days hath September . . ." Fill in the blanks with the correct month and then list the months with 31 days *before* you listen to the solution on the cassette (the order of the months is slightly different from that in the English rhyme).
(Transcript on page 110.)
Trenta giorni ha n . . . . . , con a . . . . . , g . . . . . e s . . . . . ; di ventotto ce n'è uno (f . . . . .); tutti gli altri ne han trentuno.

Exercise 2 ☆ ☐☐ (answers on the tape only)
How would you say
a A single for the 25th of August?

b A double with bathroom for the 2nd, the 3rd and the 4th of July?
c A double room with shower for fifteen days?
d Is there room for the 10th of September?
e Is it in the shade?
f Is there a restaurant?
g Do you have room for the day after tomorrow?
h We are three girls and two boys.

5 EATING OUT

KEY WORDS AND PHRASES

ci porta . . . ?	can you bring us?
il menù	the menu
l'antipasto	starters
il primo	the first course
il secondo	the second course
il contorno	vegetables or salad
il dolce	dessert
prendo	I'll have
mi porti	bring me
prendiamo	we'll have
per me	for me
per . . .	for . . .
cos'è . . . ?	what is . . . ?
le piace?	do you like?
mi piace	I like
preferisco . . .	I prefer . . .
niente dolce, grazie	no dessert, thank you
il conto	the bill

MENU A

Ristorante Al Pero – Padova

PIATTI DEL GIORNO	DISHES OF THE DAY
Zuppa di verdura	vegetable soup
Tagliatelle in brodo	tagliatelle in broth
Riso al pomodoro	rice with tomatoes
Spaghetti al ragù	what we call "spaghetti bolognese"
Spaghetti al tonno	spaghetti with tuna fish sauce

CONTORNI	SIDE DISHES
Insalata mista	mixed salad
Insalata verde	green salad

MENU B

Ristorante Da Taparo – Torreglia

ANTIPASTI

Salmone con crostino	Salmon with hot buttered toast
Prosciutto e melone	Ham and melon
Antipasto della casa	The "House" appetizer

PRIMI PIATTI

Risotto all'ortica	Nettle risotto
Risotto agli asparagi	Asparagus risotto
Risotto alla quaglia	Quail risotto
Bigoli alle salse	Home-made, thick spaghetti with a choice of sauces

Gnocchi alle salse	Small dumplings with a choice of different sauces
Zuppa di asparagi	Asparagus soup
Pappardelle agli asparagi	Asparagus pappardelle (a type of pasta)
Pasta e fagioli	Pasta and bean soup
Tagliatelle alle erbe	Herb tagliatelle

SECONDI PIATTI

Filetto alle erbe	Fillet of beef with herb sauce
Braciola di vitello	Veal chop
Braciola di maiale	Pork chop
Tagliata di manzo	Boiled beef served with sauces

DIALOGUES

ORDERING PIZZA

1

EMANUELA Ci porta cinque pizze, per favore . . . ? allora . . . una margherita, due ai funghi, una quattro stagioni senza cipolla, e una quattro stagioni con cipolla. Grazie.

ci porta will you bring us
una margherita is the basic pizza with tomato sauce and cheese
ai funghi with mushrooms
una quattro stagioni (literally a four seasons) pizza divided into four sections, with four different toppings
senza cipolla without onions

ASKING FOR THE MENU IN A *TRATTORIA*

2

GIULIA Buongiorno.
CAMERIERE Buongiorno.
GIULIA Ci porta il menù, per favore?
CAMERIERE Certo . . . Ecco a lei.
GIULIA Grazie . . . E da bere . . . una bottiglia di acqua minerale.
CAMERIERE Gassata o non gassata?
GIULIA Non gassata.
CAMERIERE Bene.
GIULIA Grazie.

ci porta il menù? will you bring us the menu?
da bere to drink
una bottiglia di acqua minerale a bottle of mineral water
gassata sparkling, an alternative to *frizzante; non gassata* still

ORDERING LUNCH

3

GIULIA Allora, un piatto di spaghetti al pomodoro, un risotto di asparagi, un'insalata verde e dei pomodori all'olio.
CAMERIERE Va bene.

un piatto di spaghetti a dish of spaghetti
al pomodoro with tomato sauce
un'insalata verde lettuce, (literally green salad)
dei pomodori all'olio sliced tomatoes dressed in olive oil
There is a list of types of pasta in the *Explanations* section for this unit.

ASKING FOR THE BILL

4

GIULIA Il conto per favore.
CAMERIERE Va bene.

il conto the bill

Exercise 1 ☆ [ ][ ] (answers on the tape only)
You are ordering lunch in a *trattoria*. Consult Menu A on page 66 for your order.

ORDERING DINNER

5

CAMERIERE I signori, che cosa prendono?
SIG. BORGHESAN Come antipasto, prendo un antipasto della casa. E come primo piatto, una zuppa di asparagi, e come secondo prendo un filetto alle erbe . . .

I signori, che cosa prendono? What will the gentleman have?
come antipasto as an appetizer/starter
prendo I will have
un antipasto della casa the restaurant's own special appetizer (*della casa,* literally of the house, of the restaurant)
come primo piatto for the first course; *il primo piatto,* the first course, is often abbreviated to *il primo*.
una zuppa di asparagi asparagus soup
come secondo for the second course; *il secondo piatto* is also abbreviated to *il secondo*.
un filetto alle erbe fillet steak in herb sauce

6

MICHELE Per me invece, del prosciutto e melone, per antipasto; gli gnocchi di patate alle salse, come primo e . . . una braciola di vitello, come secondo . . .

per me for me
invece (literally instead) on the other hand
del prosciutto e melone ham (generally Parma) with melon
gli gnocchi di patate potato dumplings
alle salse with a choice of different sauces
una braciola di vitello a veal chop

7

CAMERIERE	Un po' di insalata di contorno?
SIG. BORGHESAN	Sì.
MICHELE	Sì. Per me dell'insalata verde, grazie.
CAMERIERE	Prende del vino bianco o del vino rosso?
MICHELE	Del vino bianco secco.
SIG. BORGHESAN	Bene . . . anch'io del vino bianco secco.
CAMERIERE	Abbiamo del vino della casa, ottimo . . .
SIG. BORGHESAN	Va molto bene il vostro vino della casa.
CAMERIERE	Dell'acqua minerale?
MICHELE	Per me dell'acqua minerale gassata.
SIG. BORGHESAN	Anche per me.
CAMERIERE	Grazie.

insalata di contorno side salad as your accompanying vegetable; *contorno* is usually any vegetable served with a main course.
vino della casa house wine, also the restaurant's own home-made, or home-bottled wine
ottimo excellent
anche per me for me, too

Exercise 2 ☆ ☐☐
Consult Menu B on pages 66–67. On the tape, one of the waiters will say which of the first courses are available today. Check them off on the menu. (Transcript on page 110.)

MAKING CONVERSATION

8

MICHELE Buon appetito!
SIG. BORGHESAN Buon appetito!

9

SIG. BORGHESAN Le piace la braciola di vitello?
MICHELE Molto buona, grazie. E il suo filetto?
SIG. BORGHESAN Buonissimo.

le to you
le piace? do you like? (literally does it please to you?) *Le piace la braciola?* Do you like the chop? The reply is *sì, mi piace* yes, I like it.
molto buona very good
buonissimo excellent

ORDERING THE DESSERT

10

CAMERIERE E come dolce, che cosa prendono? Abbiamo una torta alle mele, abbiamo della torta alle mandorle, della torta alla ricotta . . .
SIG. BORGHESAN Prendo una torta alle mele.
MICHELE Per me niente dolce, grazie. Preferisco un caffè.

come dolce for dessert
torta alle mele apple tart
torta alle mandorle almond cake
torta alla ricotta a cake made with ricotta cheese
niente dolce no dessert
preferisco I prefer

EXPLANATIONS

ORDERING A MEAL

Ci porta . . . ? Will you bring us . . . ? *ci* means to us
cosa prendono i signori? what will the (ladies and) gentlemen take?, what will you have?
prendo I'll have
prendiamo we'll have

per me for me; *per la signora* for the lady; *per il signore* for the gentleman

io I; *io prendo* I'll have; *io vorrei* I would like

come primo for starters
come secondo for second course
come contorno as a side dish

cos'è? what is it? You might want to use this expression to inquire abou the name of a dish you cannot understand: *Cos'è il baccalà alla vicentina?* what is *baccalà alla vicentina?* It is a fish dish: cod boiled in oil and milk, a speciality from Vicenza. Here are other questions you may want to ask:

è carne? is it meat?
è pesce? is it fish? (beware: *pesce* fish, and not *pesche* peaches!)
è salato? is it savory/salty?
è dolce? is it sweet?
è piccante? is it spicy?
è con l'aglio? does it have garlic?

sono vegetariano (masc.)/*sono vegetariana* (fem.) I am vegetarian

non posso mangiare I cannot eat; *non posso mangiare carne* I cannot eat meat; *non posso mangiare cipolla* I cannot eat onion

le piace? do you like it? (literally is it agreeable to you?) *le piace il risotto?* do you like risotto? *le piace la pizza?* do you like pizza?

mi piace I like it; *mi piace il risotto* I like risotto
non mi piace I don't like it; *non mi piace la cipolla* I don't like onion

preferisco I prefer; *preferisco un caffè* I prefer a coffee

TYPES OF PASTA

Pasta comes in many different shapes and sizes: short, like *penne* quills or *tortiglioni;* long, like *spaghetti, tagliatelle, maccheroni, bigoli* (home-made spaghetti), *fettuccine* (thinner *tagliatelle*). Pasta for oven-baking includes *lasagne* and *cannelloni;* meat or cheese-filled pasta includes *tortellini* (with meat), *tortelloni* (bigger, filled with spinach and ricotta cheese) and *ravioli* (meat or ham).
Remember! Pasta names are always plural! *le tagliatelle, le lasagne!* If you say *la lasagna,* it means one sheet of pasta only!

Pasta dishes are served with sauces; *al pomodoro* with tomato sauce: *al ragù* what we call bolognese sauce; *al pesto* a herbal sauce made with fresh basil, pine nuts, and garlic, a speciality from Genoa. *Al, alla, ai* refer to the main ingredients of the sauce: *pizza ai funghi* pizza with mushrooms. They can also refer to the method of cooking: *al forno* oven-cooked; *ai ferri* or *alla griglia* grilled; and to the style of preparation: *pasta e fagioli alla veneta* pasta with beans in the style of the Veneto region; *saltimbocca alla romana* veal and ham cooked in the Roman style; *fegato alla veneziana* liver fried in onion and white wine, in the Venetian style, etc.

WORTH KNOWING

PLACES TO EAT

The most expensive kind of restaurant calls itself *un ristorante*. If you are looking for something cheaper, look for *una trattoria,* a small family restaurant. Sometimes, however, you can find both words together: *ristorante trattoria,* and the price can sometimes be the same as in *un ristorante. Trattorie* generally specialize in regional cooking, so they are worth trying! You can eat more cheaply in *una tavola calda,* a small self-service restaurant, or in *una rosticceria,* generally a high-quality take-out specializing in roast dishes, where it is often possible to eat on the premises. *La pizzeria* is sometimes not the most obviously cheap place to eat!

When eating in *ristoranti* or *trattorie,* avoid the *menù turistico,* the fixed-price meal, and be adventurous and try any *specialità regionale,* a dish typical of a particular region. Italian food is extremely varied, and even if you order a dish with an incomprehensible name, you are likely to eat something tasty!

An Italian meal consists generally of *il primo (piatto)* the first course, a soup, a pasta or rice dish; *il secondo (piatto)* the second course, meat or fish; *il contorno* a side dish of mixed vegetables or salad; *il dolce,* or *il dessert,* a dessert. You also have *l'antipasto* starters, which varies greatly according to the type of cuisine and restaurant: *antipasto di pesce* fish antipasto; in the menu reproduced in this unit, Sig. Borghesan asks for *un antipasto della casa* the 'house' *antipasto*. It is always advisable to try recipes, wine, etc. of the house, if on offer: *vino della casa* house wine; *dolce della casa* house dessert, etc.
coperto the cover charge
la mancia the tip

NON-PASTA DISHES

Rice dishes are typical of Northern Italy; risotto recipes are infinite! *Risotto alla quaglia* quail risotto; *risotto alla milanese* risotto with saffron in the Milanese style; *risotto agli asparagi* asparagus risotto; *risotto ai funghi* mushroom risotto, etc.

Misto often appears in the names of dishes; *insalata mista* mixed salad; *bollito misto* mixed boiled meats, served with different sauces.

Other types of meat dishes are:
braciola di maiale pork chop
braciola di vitello veal chop
cotoletta cutlet
filetto fillet
bistecca steak
pollo chicken
faraona guinea-fowl
quaglia quail
anitra duck
galletto spring chicken

Fish dishes include:
fritto misto mixed fried seafood
trota trout
zuppa di pesce fish soup
tonno tuna
seppie cuttlefish
salmone salmon

Il contorno consists generally of vegetables:
patate fritte French fries
patate arroste roast potatoes
fagiolini string beans
spinaci spinach
verdure cotte mixed boiled vegetables (spinach, fennel, artichoke, etc.)

Il dolce is the dessert and includes cakes, mousses, ice creams etc. The word also means 'cake', so you can come across *il dolce della casa,* as well as *la torta della casa.* The difference is that torta only means cake: *la torta alla ricotta* ricotta cheesecake.

Buon appetito! Bon appetit!

CAN YOU GET BY?

Exercise 1 ☐☐

Complete the following puzzle:

(Horizontal)

1 One who does not eat meat (masc.)

(Vertical)

2 Salmon is . . .

3 Beef is . . .

4 I like

5 Sweet

6 They come with the second course

	2		6		3		4			5
1										

Exercise 2 ☐☐

a one of these places is not meant for eating:
forno trattoria rosticceria tavola calda

b one of these is not meant to be eaten:
funghi pappardelle verdure cameriere

c which of these would not be a pasta dish?
lasagne bigoli alle salse tagliatelle al ragù tagliata di manzo

d which one of these would you not ask the waiter?
è piccante? è dolce o secco? senza cipolla, per favore Le piace la sua braciola di vitello?

e If you can't eat garlic, which of these dishes would be suitable for you?
torta alla ricotta pizza quattro stagioni maiale arrosto pasta al pesto

Exercise 3☆

Cos'è . . . ? You inquire about a dish you have not tried before.

Exercise 4☐☐☆

You are having a business dinner. Consult Menu B on page 66–7, and fill in the parts for both host and client.

CAMERIERA	Buonasera.
HOST	Good evening. Will you bring us the menu, please?
CAMERIERA	Subito . . . eccolo.
	(She then returns to take your order.) Cosa prendono?
CLIENT	As a starter, I'll have ham and melon.
HOST	For me too, please.
CAMERIERA	E come primo?
CLIENT	I'll have quail risotto.
CAMERIERA	È ottimo. E per lei?
HOST	For me, asparagus soup.
CAMERIERA	E poi?
CLIENT	The fillet with herbs – is it spicy?
CAMERIERA	No.
CLIENT	Then I'll have it.
CAMERIERA	Va bene. E per lei?
HOST	For me, as a second course . . . a veal chop.
CAMERIERA	Bene. Di contorno?
CLIENT	A green salad.
CAMERIERA	Anche per lei?
HOST	No – for me a mixed salad, please.

6 MEETING PEOPLE & DOING BUSINESS

KEY WORDS AND PHRASES

sono . . .	I am . . .
vorrei parlare con . . .	I'd like to speak to
il direttore	the managing director
quando torna?	when does he/she get back?
può richiamarmi?	can he/she call me back?
pronto?	hello?
ho un appuntamento con . . .	I have an appointment with
le presento	may I introduce
piacere	how do you do?
fissare un appuntamento	to arrange an appointment
la mia collega	my colleague
mia moglie	my wife
mio marito	my husband
sono occupato	I am busy
sono in ritardo	I am late
come sta?	how are you?
bene	well
di dov'è?	where are you from?
inglese	English
prenotare una macchina	to reserve a car
carta di credito	credit card
il nome è . . .	the name is . . .

DIALOGUES

MAKING A PHONE CALL

1

SEGRETARIA Zanetti Group, buongiorno.
SIG. GERMANO Buongiorno. Vorrei parlare con il direttore.
SEGRETARIA Il direttore non è in ufficio. Chi parla?
SIG. GERMANO Sono Attilio Germano, della Lori . . .

Zanetti Group is the name of the firm/company
parlare speak; *vorrei parlare con* I'd like to speak to, (literally with)
il direttore the director
non è is not; *non è in ufficio* he's not in the office
chi parla? lit. who's speaking?
sono I am
della Lori of Lori's; Lori is the name of Germano's firm (*ditta*); *della* refers to *la ditta Lori* the firm, Lori.

2

GERMANO Quando torna?
SEGRETARIA Può richiamare tra un'ora?
SIG. GERMANO Va bene, grazie.
SEGRETARIA Prego, buongiorno.
SIG. GERMANO Buongiorno.

quando torna? when is he coming back?
richiamare to call back; *può richiamare?* can you call back?
tra un'ora in an hour's time

3

SEGRETARIA	Zanetti Group, buongiorno.
GERMANO	Buongiorno. Vorrei parlare con il direttore.
SEGRETARIA	Mi dispiace, signor Germano, il direttore è occupato.
GERMANO	Può richiamarmi?
SEGRETARIA	Sì. Mi lascia il suo numero?
GERMANO	Sì. Zero sette uno novantuno tredici ottantacinque.
SEGRETARIA	Eh . . . scusi . . . può ripetere?
GERMANO	Zero sette uno novantuno tredici ottantacinque.
SEGRETARIA	La ringrazio molto, buongiorno.
GERMANO	Buongiorno.

è occupato he's busy
può richiamarmi can he call me back?
mi lascia will you leave me
novantuno ninety one
la ringrazio molto (I) thank you very much

4

SEGRETARIA	Lori, buongiorno.
ZANETTI	Il signor Germano, per favore?
SEGRETARIA	Chi devo dire?
ZANETTI	Zanetti.
SEGRETARIA	Rimanga in linea, per favore. Glielo passo subito.

chi devo dire? who should I say?
rimanga in linea hold the line
glielo passo subito I'll put him through to you immediately

Exercise 1 ☆ [ ][ ] (answer on the tape only.)
You telephone the Lori company – here is your telephone number: 044 68 48 16.

5

SEGRETARIA Buongiorno.
GERMANO Buongiorno. Sono Attilio Germano, della ditta Lori. Ho un appuntamento con il signor Zanetti.
SEGRETARIA A che ora?
GERMANO Alle cinque.
SEGRETARIA Si accomodi pure.
GERMANO Grazie.
SEGRETARIA Gli dico subito che è arrivato.

ho un appuntamento con I have an appointment with
Si accomodi pure do sit down
gli dico I'll tell him
che è arrivato that you have arrived

6

ZANETTI Il signore Germano?
GERMANO Sì.
ZANETTI Eh . . . Sono Zanetti, buongiorno.
GERMANO Piacere.
ZANETTI Le presento la mia collega, la signora Bianchi.
GERMANO Piacere.

piacere how do you do (literally pleasure, my pleasure)
le presento may I introduce, (literally I introduce to you)
la mia collega my colleague (fem.); *il mio collega* (masc.)

7

SEGRETARIA Zanetti Group, buongiorno.
GERMANO Buongiorno. Sono Attilio Germano, vorrei fissare un appuntamento con la signora Bianchi.
SEGRETARIA Attenda un attimo . . . che controllo. Domani pomeriggio va bene? . . . o . . . mercoledì?

GERMANO Ehm . . . mercoledì sono occupato. Martedì?
SEGRETARIA Martedì pomeriggio . . . va bene.
GERMANO Bene, grazie.
SEGRETARIA A che ora?
GERMANO Verso le tre?
SEGRETARIA Alle tre, va bene. D'accordo.
GERMANO Grazie, buongiorno.
SEGRETARIA Buongiorno.

fissare un appuntamento con . . . to arrange (literally to fix) an appointment with . . .
attenda un attimo . . . (please) wait a moment
che controllo . . . (literally that I check) while I check
d'accordo agreed

Exercise 2 ☆ ☐☐

Here is a page of your diary. Which day can you manage for your appointment with signora Rossi?

LUNEDÍ Roma – treno 7:45	**GIOVEDÍ** Appunt. Lori 11:30
MARTEDÍ Roma	**VENERDÍ** Pranzo 13:00
MERCOLEDÍ Ritorno treno 15:00 Appunt. Zanetti 17:00	**SABATO** —

Exercise 3 ☆ ☐☐

Record the following message on Zanetti's *segreteria telefonica* (answering machine) in Italian:

Hello, I am Vivian Stewart, the owner of Stewart Software. I'd like to arrange an appointment with the marketing director. Can he call me back? My number is 02 31 81 82 75. I am in the office tomorrow morning. Thank you, good day.

MEETING PEOPLE

8

CRISTINA	La signora Fisher?
SIG.RA FISHER	Sì . . .
CRISTINA	Sono Cristina Degani, piacere.
SIG.RA FISHER	Piacere.
CRISTINA	Mi dispiace, sono in ritardo.
SIG.RA FISHER	Non importa. Come sta?
CRISTINA	Bene, grazie. E lei?
SIG.RA FISHER	Molto bene, grazie.

mi dispiace I'm sorry
sono in ritardo I'm late
non importa (literally it isn't important) it doesn't matter
come sta? how are you?
bene well; *molto bene* very well
E lei? and you?

9

CRISTINA	Lei è tedesca?
SIG.RA FISHER	No, sono inglese.
CRISTINA	Parla molto bene l'italiano!
SIG.RA FISHER	È molto gentile.
CRISTINA	Di dov'è? Di Londra?
SIG.RA FISHER	No, sono di Cambridge. E lei?
CRISTINA	Sono di Padova.

è tedesca? are you German (fem.)?
sono inglese I'm English (masc. and fem.)
parla molto bene l'italiano you speak Italian very well
è molto gentile you are very kind
di dov'è where are you from?
di Londra from London

HIRING A CAR

10

ZANETTI	Buongiorno.
IMPIEGATO	Buongiorno.
ZANETTI	Vorrei prenotare una macchina.
IMPIEGATO	Che tipo di macchina?
ZANETTI	Un'utilitaria.
IMPIEGATO	Va bene una . . . Fiat Panda?
ZANETTI	Va bene.
IMPIEGATO	Per quanto tempo?
ZANETTI	Una settimana.
IMPIEGATO	Che giorno le serve?
ZANETTI	Dal 26 maggio.
IMPIEGATO	Per sette giorni.
ZANETTI	Sì.
IMPIEGATO	Costa più o meno centomila lire al giorno.
ZANETTI	Va bene. Posso pagare con una carta di credito?
IMPIEGATO	Sì, può pagare con qualsiasi carta di credito: American Express, VISA, oppure la nostra carta di credito Hertz.
ZANETTI	Grazie.

vorrei prenotare una macchina I would like to reserve a car
che tipo di macchina? what kind of car?
un'utilitaria a small car
per quanto tempo? for how long?
una settimana a week
che giorno le serve? what day do you need it for?
dal 26 maggio from May 26
per sette giorni for seven days
più o meno more or less
al giorno per day
posso pagare con una carta di credito? may I pay with a credit card?

con qualsiasi carta di credito with any credit card
oppure or
la nostra carta our (credit) card

11

ZANETTI	Buongiorno. Ho prenotato una macchina.
IMPIEGATO	Buongiorno. A che nome?
ZANETTI	Zanetti.
IMPIEGATO	Ha la patente, per cortesia?
ZANETTI	Sì, eccola.
IMPIEGATO	Ha la carta di credito?
ZANETTI	Sì, la VISA.
IMPIEGATO	Molto bene.

ho prenotato una macchina I have reserved a car
a che nome? under what name?
ha la patente? have you got your driving license?

Exercise 4 ☆
You rent a car.

EXPLANATIONS

INTRODUCING YOURSELF

sono I am: *sono Zanetti* (literally I am Zanetti) my name is Zanetti; *il nome è* the name is.

ADDRESSING PEOPLE

signor, signora, signorina
Signor is used without the article when addressing a man, and is always followed by the surname: *signor Zanetti, signor Borghesan*. So, *Buongiorno, signor Borghesan* Hello Mr. Borghesan.

But, *vorrei parlare con* ***il*** *signor Borghesan* I'd like to speak to Mr. Borghesan. *Signore* is only used without the surname when addressing somebody you do not know: *scusi, signore?* excuse me, sir?
Signora and *signorina* follow the same rule:
Buongiorno, signora Bianchi
Buonasera, signorina Degani but *ho un appuntamento con* ***la*** *signora Bianchi, vorrei parlare con* ***la*** *signorina Degani.*
Note that *signorina,* although still common as a title and an address, is used mainly with very young women.

INTRODUCING OTHER PEOPLE

Le presento May I introduce? *Le presento la mia collega* May I introduce my colleague?

il direttore the managing director of a firm
la ditta the firm, the company
il direttore della vendite the marketing director
il vice-direttore the assistant manager
il titolare (masc.), *la titolare* (fem.) the owner of the firm
mio, mia my
la mia collega my colleague (fem.); *il mio collega* (masc.) *il mio direttore*
To translate 'my' with words defining a close relative, drop *il, la* etc:
mio marito my husband
mia moglie my wife
mio figlio my son
mia figlia my daughter

piacere (literally my pleasure) how do you do

BEING POLITE

come sta? how are you?
bene well
sto bene I am well
e lei? and you?

DI DOV'È?

di dov'è? where are you from?
sono di . . . I am from . . . *sono di Torino* I am from Turin; if you want to say which country you come from, the easiest way is to say that you are English, American, Italian, etc.:
sono inglese I am English
gallese Welsh
scozzese Scottish
irlandese Irish
francese French
canadese Canadian

britannico (masc.), *britannica* (fem.) British
tedesco (masc.), *tedesca* (fem.) German
italiano (masc.), *italiana* (fem.) Italian
americano (masc.) *americana* (fem.) American
australiano (masc.) *australiana* (fem.) Australian

MAKING APPOINTMENTS

un appuntamento an appointment
fissare un appuntamento to make an appointment
vorrei fissare un appuntamento con . . . I'd like to make an appointment with . . .
ho un appuntamento I have an appointment

USING THE PHONE

pronto? hello?
chi parla? who's speaking?
chi devo dire? who should I say?
come si chiama? what is your name? (literally how are you called?)
il nome è . . . the name is . . .

Here are some answers you might get when you are trying to contact somebody:
è occupato he is busy; *è occupata* she is busy

non è in sede he/she is not at the head office
non è in ufficio he/she is not in the office
è fuori he/she is out

la segreteria telefonica the answering machine (Note: *segretaria* is secretary.)
siamo temporaneamente assenti we are temporarily absent from the office

And here is what you might need to say:
sono occupato/a I am busy
ho un impegno I have a commitment
non posso I can't; *giovedì non posso* I can't make it on Thursday
può richiamarmi? can he/she call me back?; if you want to ask 'when can I call back?', you say *quando posso richiamare?*
quando torna? when does he/she get back?
mi dispiace, sono in ritardo I am sorry, I am late

THE ALPHABET

You will almost certainly have to spell your name when you are in Italy. The spelling in Italian is done using the names of cities, rather than of people or things, as in English: *R come Roma, M come Milano,* etc. Here is the complete list; listen to the tape for the pronunciation of the letters.

A come Ancona
B come Bologna
C come Como
D come Domodossola
E come Empoli
F come Firenze
G come Genova
H come Hotel
I come Imola
J come Jersey
K come Kilo
L come Livorno
M come Milano
N come Napoli
O come Otranto
P come Palermo
Q come Quaderno (notebook)
R come Roma
S come Savona
T come Torino
U come Udine
V come Venezia

W come Washington
X ics
Y come York
Z come Zurigo

WORTH KNOWING

TRAVELING BY CAR

Gasoline in Italy is sold by the liter, *al litro.* Ask for *il pieno* if you want to fill the tank. If you want to save money you can pay with coupons, which you can obtain from any branch of the *Automobile Club d'Italia (ACI).* They will give you any information relevant to your license, insurance, etc., in connection with Italian law, and they will also carry out emergency breakdown services on any roads.
gasoline is *benzina;* lead-free gas is *benzina senza piombo (verde* green).

Motorways in Italy are *a pagamento* toll roads; you can get a *viacard,* a credit card which you can use to pay *al casello* at the tollbooth. It can be purchased from any ACI branch, but also from service stations and even tobacconists. The symbol for thruways is a black number, preceded by *A* for *Autostrada,* on a green background.
Main roads are marked by the symbol *SS (strada statale* state road); *tangenziale* or *circonvallazione* is the ring road:
tangenziale est east-bound ring road; *ovest* west; *nord* north; *sud* south
If you want to rent a car, look for the sign *Autonoleggio* (car rental) at the airport, or at the railway station. The categories of cars vary from firm to firm, but if you want a small car, ask for *un'utilitaria,* or for *un'economica.* You will be given *un contratto* a contract, outlining the general agreement *(le condizioni generali).* To rent a car you need to be 21, and 23 to hire some of the most expensive, or biggest cars. The fee may or may not include IVA *(Imposta sul valore aggiunto,* i.e. VAT).

CAN YOU GET BY?

Exercise 1 ☐☐

1 In answer to which of the following questions would you not give your name?

a A che nome?
b Come si chiama?
c Chi parla?
d Chi devo dire?
e Come sta?

2 You are unlikely to go out for dinner with one of the following:

a titolare
b direttore
c segreteria telefonica
d segretaria

3 Which of the following would you not say when making an appointment?

a Giovedì non posso.
b Sono in ufficio domani.
c Non è in sede.
d Alle tre ho un impegno.

Exercise 2 ☆

You arrive late for an appointment.

Exercise 3 ☆☐☐

Listen to the recording of the Hertz employee summarizing the contract, and then fill in the details in the form provided opposite. (Transcript on page 112.)

AUTONOLEGGIO			
AUTO	N°GIORNI	DATA	TARIFFA
		DAL....AL....	£.....(IVA esclusa) £.....tutto incluso

Exercise 4 ☆
You receive a business call.

REFERENCE SECTION

PRONUNCIATION

The best way to develop a good pronunciation is to listen carefully to the dialogues on the cassettes, to repeat words and phrases, and to do the exercises until you are fluent. This brief guide only deals with the basics of Italian pronunciation.

Vowels in Italian are a little different from English ones; they are more 'open', and have fewer variations than the English ones:

A sounds like the 'u' in bunk: *banca, pasta*
E is like the 'e' in bet: *va bene, bicchiere*
I is like the 'ea' in tea: *vino*
O is like the 'o' in lot: *otto*
U is like the 'oo' in pool: *una*

Difficult sounds:
C followed by A, O, U or other consonants is a hard sound, as in cut, cat, etc: *cameriere, banca.*
C followed by E or I is soft, like 'ch' in church: *cento, arrivederci, cioccolata.*
CH is a hard sound: *pesche* (peaches)
G is also hard when followed by A, O, U: *albergo,* or by another consonant, *grande;* it is soft when followed by E or I: *Genova, giugno*
GH is a hard sound: *alberghi.*

GL is like 'lli' in million: *luglio, biglietto.*
GN is like 'ni' in onion: *signore, giugno, Gran Bretagna.*

H before a vowel is always mute: *ha, hanno* (pronounced A as the 'a' in *banca*).
QU is like 'qu' in quick: *quanto, quale.*
Z is either like the 'ts' in cats: *colazione,* or 'ds' as in lads: *zero, zucchero.*

STRESS

In many words, stress falls on the next-to-last syllable: *passa*por*to, bigli*et*to, staz*ione, etc. but this is not always the case: le*ttera,* gra*zie,* ta*volo, etc.*
Words that end with an accented vowel must be pronounced with a strong stress on that vowel:
*caff*è, *dov'*è, *citt*à.

VERBS

Verbs in this course are taught as part of key phrases, and not by themselves, as you can get by without learning them properly. However, here are some basic ones, in all their forms, including the familiar *tu* forms which are not taught in this course:

to be	sono	I am
	sei	you are (familiar form)
	è	he/she/it is; you are (polite forms; *c'è* there is)
	siamo	we are
	siete	you are (plural)
	sono	they are (*ci sono* there are)

to have	ho	I have
	hai	you have (familiar form)
	ha	he/she/it has; you have (polite form)
	abbiamo	we have
	avete	you have (plural)
	hanno	they have
to speak	parlo	I speak
	parli	you speak (familiar form)
	parla	he/she speaks; you (polite) speak
	parliamo	we speak
	parlate	you (plural) speak
	parlano	they speak

Italian does not use the words for 'I,' 'you,' etc., very often because the verb forms indicate which person is doing what; you have come across *io* (I) and *lei,* you (polite form). The word for the familiar form of you is *tu*. It is used with family, friends, and people you call by their first name; it would be considered impolite to use it with anybody else, especially with people you have never met before.

NEGATIVES

To make the verb negative, you only need to put *non* in front of it: *non posso* I can't; *non mi piace* I don't like it; *non ho capito* I haven't understood.

NUMBERS

0 zero	11 undici	22 ventidue
1 uno	12 dodici	23 ventitré
2 due	13 tredici	24 ventiquattro

3 tre
4 quattro
5 cinque
6 sei
7 sette
8 otto
9 nove
10 dieci

14 quattordici
15 quindici
16 sedici
17 diciassette
18 diciotto
19 diciannove
20 venti
21 ventuno

25 venticinque
26 ventisei
27 ventisette
28 ventotto
29 ventinove
30 trenta
31 trentuno
32 trentadue
33 trentatré
etc.

40 quaranta
50 cinquanta
60 sessanta
70 settanta
80 ottanta
90 novanta
100 cento
101 centoeuno
102 centodue
200 duecento

300 trecento
400 quattrocento
500 cinquecento
600 seicento
700 settecento
800 ottocento
900 novecento
1000 mille
2000 duemila
10,000 diecimila
100,000 centomila
1,000,000 milione

LANGUAGE NOTES

Further and more detailed language notes can be found in the *Explanations* section of each unit.

Masculine and feminine	Unit 1
il and *la* *del* plurals *questo, questa*	Unit 2

dove, dov'è? Telling the time	Unit 3
Dates Days of the week Months of the year	Unit 4
Cos'è? *mi piace*	Unit 5
Introductions Politeness Making appointments The alphabet	Unit 6

TEMPERATURE CONVERSIONS

To change Fahrenheit to Centigrade, subtract 32 and multiply by ⅝.
To change Centigrade to Fahrenheit, multiply by ⅝ and add 32.

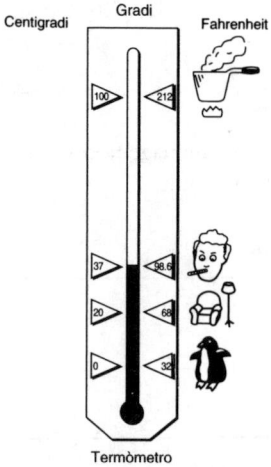

WEIGHTS AND MEASURES

Centimeters/Inches

It is usually unnecessary to make exact conversions from your customary inches to the metric system used in Italy, but to give you an approximate idea of how they compare, we give you the following guide.

To convert **centimetri** into inches, multiply by .39.

To convert inches into **centimetri,** multiply by 2.54.

Centimetri

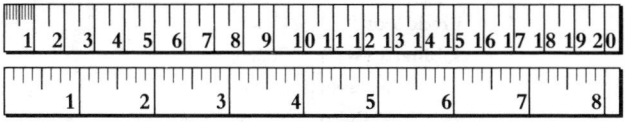

Pollici

Meters / Feet

1 meter **(metro)** = 39.37 inches
= 3.28 feet
= 1.09 yards

1 foot = 0.3 meters
1 yard = 0.9 meters

Kilograms / Pounds

1 kilogram **(chilo)** = 2.2 pounds
1 pound = 0.45 kilogram

Liters / Quarts

1 liter = 1.06 quarts
4 liters = 1.06 gallons

For quick approximate conversion, multiply the number of gallons by 4 to get liters **(litri).** Divide the number of liters by 4 to get gallons.

IMPORTANT SIGNS

Acqua (non)potabile	(Not) potable water
Alt	Stop
Aperto	Open
Attenzione	Caution, watch out
Avanti	Enter (come in, go, walk [at the lights])
Caldo or "C"	Hot
Chiuso	Closed
Divieto di sosta	No parking
Divieto di transito	No entrance, keep out
Freddo or "F"	Cold
Gabinetti (WC)	Toilets
Ingresso	Entrance
Libero	Vacant
Non toccare	Hands off, don't touch
Occupato	Occupied
Pericolo	Danger
Riservato	Reserved
Si vende	For sale
Signora	Women's room
Signore	Men's room
Spingere	Push
Tirare	Pull
Uscita	Exit
Vietato fumare	No smoking

ROAD SIGNS

Guarded railroad crossing

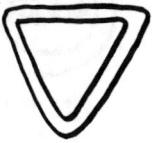

Yield

Stop

Right of way

Dangerous intersection ahead

Gasoline (petrol) ahead

Parking

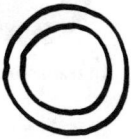

No vehicles allowed

Dangerous curve

Pedestrian crossing

Oncoming traffic has right of way

No bicycles allowed

No parking allowed

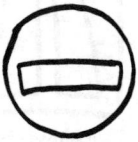

No entry

No left turn

No U-turn

No passing

Border crossing

Traffic signal ahead

Speed limit

Traffic circle (roundabout) ahead

Minimum speed limit

All traffic turns left

End of no passing zone

One-way street

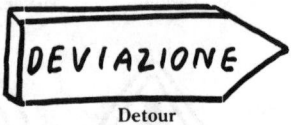

Detour

Danger ahead

Entrance to expressway

Expressway ends

MENU ITEMS

Appetizers (Starters)

Antipasti mostly consist of raw salads, cooked chilled vegetables dressed with a vinaigrette, and massive varieties of sausages and salamis. Some key terms are:

acciughe	*ah-chee-OH-gheh*	anchovies
antipasto misto	*ahn-tee-pAHs-toh mEEs-toh*	assorted appetizers
carciofi	*kahr-chee-OH-fee*	artichoke
mortadella	*mohr-tah-dEHl-lah*	cold sausage, similar to bologna
prosciutto crudo	*proh-shee-OOt-toh krOO-doh*	raw cured ham
tartufi	*tahr-tOO-fee*	truffles (white)

Soups

Soups can be either thick or thin, and thus are given different names. **Brodi** are generally broths, while **zuppe** are thick and hearty.

brodo di manzo	*brOH-doh dee mAHn-tsoh*	broth, generally meat-based
brodo di pollo	*brOH-hod dee pOHl-loh*	chicken broth
brodo magro di vegetali	*brOH-doh mAH-groh dee veh-jeh-tAH-lee*	vegetable broth
crema di ____	*krEH-mah dee*	creamed ____ soup
cacciucco	*kah-chee-OO-koh*	seafood chowder
minestra in brodo	*mee-nEHs-trah een brOH-doh*	pasta in broth
minestrone	*mee-nehs-trOH-neh*	thick vegetable soup
zuppa di ____	*tsOOp-pah dee*	thick soup

Entrees (Meat and Fish Dishes)

The "main course" of an Italian meal is usually either a sautéed or grilled meat or a baked fish or chicken. Along the coast you'll find unusual varieties of seafood.

acciughe	*ah-chee-OO-gheh*	anchovies
anguille	*ahn-goo-EEl-leh*	eel
aragosta	*ah-rah-gOHs-tah*	lobster (spiny)
baccalà	*bah-kah-lAH*	dried salt cod
branzino (nasello)	*brahn-tsEE-noh (nah-sEHl-loh)*	bass (hake)
calamari (seppie)	*kah-lah-mAH-ree (sAYp-pee-eh)*	squid
cozze	*kOH-tseh*	mussels
gamberetti	*gAHm-beh-rAY-tee*	prawns
granchi	*grAHn-key*	crabs
lumache	*loo-mAH-keh*	snails
merluzzo	*mayr-lOOt-tsoh*	cod
ostriche	*OHs-tree-keh*	oysters
polipo	*pOH-lee-poh*	octopus
salmone	*sahl-mOH-neh*	salmon
sardine	*sahr-dEE-neh*	sardines
scampi	*skAHm-pee*	shrimps
sogliola	*sOH-ly-ee-oh-lah*	flounder (sole)
trota	*trOH-tah*	trout
tonno	*tOHn-noh*	tuna
vongole	*vOHn-goh-leh*	clams
trance di pesce alla griglia	*trAHn-chee dee pAY-sheh AHl-lah grEE-ly-ee-ah*	grilled fish steaks
fritto misto di pesce	*frEEt-toh mEEs-toh dee pAY-sheh*	mixed fried fish

Meat dishes are often sauced or served with gravy.

agnello (abbacchio)	*ah-ny-EHl-loh (ahb-bAH-key-oh)*	lamb
capretto	*kah-prAYy-toh*	goat
maiale	*mah-ee-AH-leh*	pork
manzo	*mAHn-tsoh*	beef
montone	*mohn-tOH-neh*	mutton
vitello	*vee-tEHl-loh*	veal

Some common cuts of meat, plus other menu terms:

affettati	*ahf-fayt-tAH-tee*	cold cuts
anitra	*AH-nee-trah*	duck
costate	*kohs-tAH-teh*	chops
animelle	*ah-nee-mEHl-leh*	sweetbreads
cervello	*chehr-vEHl-loh*	brains
fegato	*fAY-gah-toh*	liver
bistecca	*bees-tAY-kah*	steak
lingua	*lEEn-goo-ah*	tongue
pancetta	*pahn-chAYt-tah*	bacon
pollo	*pOHl-loh*	chicken
polpette	*pohl-pAYt-teh*	meatballs
prosciutto	*proh-shee-OOt-toh*	ham
rognoni	*roh-ny-OH-nee*	kidneys
tacchino	*tah-kEY-noh*	turkey

Vegetables

asparagi	*ahs-pAH-rah-jee*	asparagus
carciofi	*kahr-chee-OH-fee*	artichoke
carote	*kah-rOH-teh*	carrots
cavoli	*kAH-voh-lee*	cabbage
cavolfiori	*kah-vohl-fee-OH-ree*	cauliflower

cetriolo	*cheh-tree-OO-loh*	cucumber
ceci	*chay-chee*	chick-peas
fagioli	*fah-jee-oh-lEE*	beans (dried)
fagiolini	*fah-jee-oh-lEE-nee*	green beans
funghi	*fOOn-ghee*	mushrooms
lattuga	*laht-tOO-gah*	lettuce
lenticchie	*len-tEE-key-eh*	lentils
melanzana	*meh-lAHn-tsah-nah*	eggplant
peperoni	*peh-peh-rOH-nee*	pepper
patate	*pah-tAH-teh*	potatoes
piselli	*pee-sEHl-lee*	peas
pomodoro	*poh-moh-dOH-roh*	tomato
porcini	*pohr-chee-nee*	wild mushroom
sedano	*sAY-dah-noh*	celery
spinaci	*spee-nAH-chee*	spinach

Fruits

albicocca	*ahl-bee-kOH-kah*	apricot
ananasso	*ah-nah-nAHs-soh*	pineapple
arancia	*ah-rAHn-chee-ah*	orange
ciliege	*chee-lee-EH-jee-eh*	cherries
fragole	*frAH-goh-leh*	strawberries
lampone	*lahm-pOH-neh*	raspberry
limone	*lee-mOH-neh*	lemon
mela	*mAY-lah*	apple
melone	*meh-LOH-neh*	melon
pera	*pAY-rah*	pear
pesca	*pAYS-kah*	peach
pompelmo	*pohm-pEHl-moh*	grapefruit
prugne	*prOO-ny-eh*	plum
uva	*OO-vah*	grape

KEY TO EXERCISES

1 SAYING HELLO AND ORDERING DRINKS

Exercise 1

Transcript:

SERGIO	Allora . . . due più tre . . .	2+3
DAUGHTER	Cinque.	5
SERGIO	Tre più tre . . .	3+3
DAUGHTER	Sei.	6
SERGIO	Dieci meno cinque . . .	10–5
DAUGHTER	Cinque.	5
SERGIO	Cinque più tre . . .	5+3
DAUGHTER	Otto.	8
SERGIO	Otto più due . . .	8+2
DAUGHTER	Dieci.	10
SERGIO	Due . . . più quattro . . .	2+4
DAUGHTER	Sei.	6
SERGIO	Nove più uno . . .	9+1
DAUGHTER	Dieci.	10
SERGIO	Uno più uno . . .	1+1
DAUGHTER	Due.	2

Exercise 2

Transcript:

a Il telefono è nove nove zero zero zero uno zero (9900010).

b Se vuole il numero di telefono? Allora, cinque due nove uno uno zero otto (5291108).

c Il numero di telefono? Allora: otto due zero nove sette undici (8209711).

Exercise 4

Transcript:

MICHELE — Eh . . . il Brachetto è un vino bianco o rosso?

CAMERIERE — Il Brachetto è un vino rosso dolce.

MICHELE — Ah, bene. Allora, due bicchieri di Brachetto e . . . vino bianco secco?

CAMERIERE — Vino bianco secco . . . potrei darle del Soave.

MICHELE — Bene. Allora, due bicchieri di Brachetto e tre bicchieri di Soave.

VINO	BIANCO	ROSSO	DOLCE	SECCO
Brachetto		✓	✓	
Soave	✓			✓

CAN YOU GET BY?

Exercise 1 Word search

U	E	**B**	S	T	**E**	**I**	**Z**	**A**	**R**	**G**	O	M	P
L	N	**U**	A	R	P	C	C	D	F	H	A	N	Y
B	**U**	**O**	**N**	**G**	**I**	**O**	**R**	**N**	**O**	A	L	E	S
L	O	**N**	A	D	F	E	L	P	Q	S	U	I	T
O	L	**A**	R	T	D	D	S	O	A	F	I	L	R
R	I	**S**	T	O	**P**	**E**	**R**	**F**	**A**	**V**	**O**	**R**	**E**
Q	P	**E**	A	N	R	V	O	E	B	B	C	D	I
A	**P**	**R**	**E**	**G**	**O**	I	D	Z	Z	F	P	N	U
L	A	**A**	E	R	I	R	D	O	Z	P	S	V	V
V	L	Z	P	D	R	R	I	A	A	E	Q	P	Q
V	U	E	E	L	**O**	**A**	**I**	**C**	R	S	V	Z	H

Exercise 2
Bingo card, 600 *seicento* has not been called.

Exercise 3
1b, 2b, 3c, 4a, 5b

2 SHOPPING

Exercise 3
Transcript: Abbiamo: eh . . . fragola, limone, pistacchio, pesca, pera, pompelmo, mirtillo, ananas. Poi abbiamo: stracciatella, nocciola, cioccolato, yogurt, tiramisù, panna e vaniglia.
Translation: We have: strawberry, lemon, pistachio, peach, pear, grapefruit, blueberry, pineapple. Then we have: chocolate chip, hazelnut, chocolate, yogurt, *tiramisù* (lit., pick-me-up, a Venetian sweet), cream and vanilla.
Key: yes, he does: pesca and cioccolato.

CAN YOU GET BY?

Exercise 2
Transcript: Tremilasettecentocinquanta 3,750 lire
Ottomila lire 8,000 lire
Quattromilanovecinquanta 4,950
Trentamila 30,000
Ventiduemiladuecento lire 22,200 lire.

Exercise 3
1b, 2b, 3c, 4c, 5b

3 TRAVELING AROUND

Exercise 2
a Un'andata per Roma, per favore

b Due biglietti di andate e ritorno per Napoli in prima classe
c Venezia, andata e ritorno, con supplemento rapido

Exercise 3
Le cinque e mezza 5:30
mezzogiorno meno un quarto 11:45
l'una e dieci 1:10
le dodici e venti 12:20
le diciotto e quaranta 18:40 (6:40)
mezzanotte meno cinque 11:55

Exercise 4
Timetable: the train leaves Milan at 7:55; it arrives at Bologna at 9:42; the connection is at 10:00; it arrives in Florence at 10:46.

IL RITORNO DA MILANO-BOLOGNA PER FIRENZE

PARTENZA

											Exp					
Milano C.Le	p	0:15									7:55	8:55	9:55	10:32		12:45
Bologna	p	2:59	3:37	5:07	5:42	6:00	6:08	6:52	7:42	7:54	10:00	10:42	11:42	12:42	13:27	14:14

ARRIVO

Firenze SMN	a		4:55	6:26	6:46	7:13		8:27	8:47	9:06	10:46	11:46	12:46	13:46	14:32	

CAN YOU GET BY?

Exercise 1
Transcript: Allora, di mattina dalle nove alle dodici e trenta . . . dalle nove alle dodici e trenta. E di pomeriggio, dalle quattordici alle diciannove . . . dalle quattordici alle diciannove.
Key: From 14:00 till 19:00.

Exercise 2
1b, 2c, 3b, 4c

4 GETTING SOMEWHERE TO STAY

Exercise 3

Transcript: Una camera doppia costa centoeunmila lire, esclusa la colazione. Eh, la colazione costa tredicimila lire a persona. Eh, una camera singola costa sessantottomila lire, esclusa la colazione, e . . . tutte le camere hanno i servizi e la doccia. Le camere matrimoniali hanno la vasca da bagno e costano centoeottomila lire, esclusa la colazione.

Key: 101,000 lire + 13,000 + 13,000 = 127,000

Exercise 4

Transcript: due ragazzi e una ragazza; un ragazzo e tre ragazze; tre ragazze e quattro ragazzi; quattro ragazze e due ragazzi.

26 MAGGIO	RAGAZZI	RAGAZZE
	2	1
	1	3
	4	3
	2	4

Exercise 6

Transcript: Da gennaio a febbraio, sono a Londra . . .
Da marzo a luglio, sono a Roma per un film . . .
Da agosto a settembre, sono a Venezia . . .
In ottobre, vado in America per due mesi . . .
Torno a Londra in dicembre . . .

CAN YOU GET BY?

Exercise 1

Transcript: Trenta giorni ha novembre, con aprile, giugno e settembre; di ventotto ce n'è uno (febbraio); tutti gli altri ne han trentuno.

Translation: Thirty days hath November, with April, June and September; there's one with twenty eight (days) (February); all the others have thirty one (days).

5 EATING OUT

Exercise 2

Transcript: Come primo piatto abbiamo; delle pappardelle, agli asparagi freschi. Abbiamo una zuppa, agli asparagi. Ci sono i gnocchi di patate, alle salse; i bigoli – sono gli spaghetti grossi, fatti in casa, alle salse. Ci sono i risotti, agli asparagi, all'ortica, alla quaglia . . .

Translation: As first course we have: *pappardelle* (a type of pasta) with fresh asparagus sauce. We have a soup, of asparagus. There are potato *gnocchi* with a choice of different sauces; *bigoli* – they're the thick, home-made spaghetti, with different sauces. There are risottos with asparagus, nettles, quail . . .

CAN YOU GET BY?

Exercise 1

Here is the solved puzzle.

	[2] P		[6] V		[3] C		[4] M			[5] D
[1] V	E	G	E	T	A	R	I	A	N	O
	S		R		R		P			L
	C		D		N		I			C
	E		U		E		A			E
			R				C			
			E				E			

Exercise 2

a forno, **b** cameriere, **c** tagliata di manzo, **d** Le piace la sua braciola di vitello? **e** torta alla ricotta

6 MEETING PEOPLE AND DOING BUSINESS

Exercise 2

Transcript: La signora Rossi è libera martedì alle undici, mercoledì alle sedici e trenta e giovedì alle quindici e trenta. Quando le va bene?

Key: Giovedì alle quindici e trenta (Thursday at 15:30).

Exercise 3

Translation: Buongiorno. Sono Vivian Stewart. Sono la titolare della ditta Stewart Software. Vorrei fissare un appuntamento con il direttore delle vendite. Può richiamarmi? Il mio numero è zero due . . . tre uno . . . otto uno . . . otto due . . . sette cinque. Sono in ufficio domani mattina. Grazie, buongiorno.

CAN YOU GET BY?

Exercise 1
1e, 2c, 3c

Exercise 3
Transcript: Ecco. Questo è il contratto. Lei ha noleggiato una macchina dal 15 di agosto fino al 30 di agosto, per quindici giorni, a centomila lire al giorno; è una Fiat Uno, tutto incluso.
Translation: Here (it is). This is the contract. You have rented a car from August 15 to August 30, for fifteen days, at 100,000 lire per day; it's a Fiat Uno, everything included.

AUTONOLEGGIO			
AUTO	N°GIORNI	DATA	TARIFFA
Fiat Uno	15	DAL15/8 AL 30/8	£.....(IVA esclusa) £100,000 tutto incluso

WORD LIST

ITALIAN-ENGLISH

All translations given are as used in this book. Bold type shows where the stress falls in each word.
Abbreviations: M. = masculine, f. = feminine, sing. = singular, pl. = plural.
Adjectives are listed with their masculine and feminine endings (freddo, -a) . . .

A

a at, to
*abbi**am**o* we have
ac**com**odi: *s'ac**com**odi* please go to, please sit down
l' ***a**cqua* (f.) water
l' ***a**cqua mine**ra**le* mineral water; *l'**a**cqua mine**ra**le gas**sa**ta* (or *friz**zan**te*) sparkling mineral water; *l'**a**cqua mine**ra**le* non gas**sa**ta (or *natu**ra**le*) regular mineral water
l' ***adul**to* (m.) adult
l' ***agl**io* (m.) garlic
ai (= a + i) at/to the
*ai **fun**ghi* with mushrooms
al (= a + il) at/to the; *al **la**tte/li**mon**e* with milk/lemon; *al se**ma**foro* at the lights; *al **ton**no* with tuna fish sauce
l' *al**ber**go* hotel; *l'albergat**o**re* (m.), *l'albergat**ri**ce*

(f.) hotelier
all' (= a + l')
alla (= a + la) at/to the, in the style of . . . : *alla quaglia* with quail; *alla vicentina* in the style of Vicenza
alle (= a + le) (+ time) at . . .
allora now then
americano, -a American
anche too, also
andare to go: *per andare a . . . ?* the way to . . . ?
andata one-way: *andata e ritorno* round-trip
l' *anitra* (f.) duck
l' *antipasto* (m.) starter
aperto, -a open
appetito appetite: *buon appetito* bon appetit
l' *appuntamento* (m.) appointment
arance oranges
l' *aranciata* (f.) orangeade
l' *aria condizionata* (f.) air conditioning
arrivederci goodbye
l' *arrivo* (m.) arrival
l' *ascensore* (m.) lift
assenti (pl.) absent
australiano, -a Australian
l' *autobus* (m.) bus
l' *autoleggio* (m.) car rental/lease
l' *autostrada* (f.) thruway
avete do you (pl.) have?

B

il *bagno* bath
il *bambino* child
la *banca* bank
il *bar* bar

basta enough: *basta così?* is that enough? is that all?
basta, grazie that's all, thanks
bene well: *va bene* OK, fine; *benissimo* very well, very good
la benzina gasoline
bere to drink: *qualcosa da bere* something to drink
bianco, -a white
il bicchiere glass
la biglietteria ticket office
il biglietto ticket
il binario platform
la birra beer
la bistecca steak
la borsetta handbag
la bottiglia bottle
la braciola chop
la brioche bun
britannico, -a British
buonanotte goodnight
buonasera hello, good evening
buongiorno hello, good morning
buonissimo, -a excellent
buono, -a good
il burro butter

C

il caffè coffee: *il caffè lungo* weaker black coffee; *il caffè macchiato* coffee with a dash of milk
cambiare to change: *posso cambiare . . . ?* can I change . . . ?
il cambio exchange
la camera bedroom
il campeggio campsite
canadese (m. and f.) Canadian

la cantina wine shop
capito understood: *non ho capito* I didn't understand
il cappuccino espresso with steamed milk
la carne meat
caro, -a expensive
la carta di credito credit card
la carta telefonica phone card
la cartolina postcard
la cassa till, till counter
c'è there is
il centro centre: *il centro città* city center
certo certainly
che that, what, which? *a che ore?* at what time? *da che binario?* from which platform?
chi? who? *chi devo dire?* who shall I say?
la chiave key
il chilo kilo
chiuso, -a closed
ciao hello, hi, bye
la cipolla onion
la città city, town
la classe class: *prima classe* first class
la coincidenza connection
la colazione breakfast
il/ la collega colleague
come as, like: *come primo* as first course; *come si chiama?* what is your name? (polite form); *come sta?* how are you? (polite form)
completo: al completo fully booked
con with
continua you continue: *continua sempre dritto* you continue straight on (polite form)
il conto bill
il contorno vegetables or salad (side dish)

il contratto contract
corrente: la presa di corrente electrical outlet
cosa what: *cosa prendono?* what will you have?;
cos'è? what is (it)?
costa it costs: *quanto costa?* how much does it cost?
cotto, -a cooked
crudo, -a raw; cured: *prosciutto crudo* cured ham (e.g., Parma)

D

da from: *da bere* to drink; *d'accordo* agreed, OK; *da cinquemila* five thousand (lire) worth
dal (= da + il) *binario quattro* from platform (number) four
dalle (da + le) *due* from 2 o'clock
dei (= di + i) any, some: *dei gettoni* any, some telephone tokens
del (di + il) any, some: *ha del formaggio?* do you have any cheese?
desidera? may I help you?
la destinazione destination
destra right: *a destra* to the right; *sulla destra* on the right
di of
la diarrea diarrhea
il diretto train that has designated stops
il direttore the managing director: *il direttore delle vendite* the marketing director
dispiace: mi dispiace I'm sorry
la doccia shower
il documento document
il dolce dessert
il dollaro dollar
domani tomorrow

domenica Sunday
dopo after
dopodomani the day after tomorrow
doppia: camera doppia twin-bedded room
dove? where? *dov'è?* where is?
dritto straight on
il duomo cathedral

E

e and
è is
ecco here is . . . : *ecco il caffè* here is the coffee; *èccoli* here they are
esclusa: IVA esclusa VAT excluded
l' espresso (m.) small black coffee
etto 100 grams

F

fagioli beans
fagiolini string beans
la farmacia pharmacy
le ferie holiday
chiuso per ferie closed for vacation
la fermata bus stop
la fiera trade fair
il filetto fillet
fino as far as, to, until: *fino al semaforo* as far as the (traffic) light; *fino alle due* until 2 o'clock
firmare to sign: *può firmare?* can you sign?
fissare to arrange
il formaggio cheese
il forno oven: *al forno* oven-heated
la fragola strawberry

francese (m. and f.) French
il francobollo stamp
fritto, -a fried
la frutta fruit
il fruttivendolo fruitseller
fumatori: fumatori o non fumatori? smoking or non-smoking?
funghi mushrooms
fuori out, outside: *fuori della stazione* outside the station

G

gallese (m. and f.) Welsh
gassata: acqua minerale gassata sparkling mineral water
il gelato ice cream
gentile kind: *è molto gentile* you (polite form) are very kind
il gettone telephone token
il giorno day: *al giorno* per day
il giovedì Thursday
giri turn: *giri a sinistra* turn left
giusto? is that right?
le gocce drops (medicinal)
la Gran Bretagna Great Britain
grazie thank you
il gusto flavor

H

ha he/she has; you have (polite form): *ha del formaggio?* do you have any cheese?
ho I have: *non ho capito* I didn't understand

I

I the (m. pl.)
ieri yesterday
il the (m. sing.)
l' impegno (m.) commitment
l' impiegato (m.) employee
importa: non importa it doesn't matter
in in
incluso included: *tutto incluso* everything included
informazioni (pl.) information: *informazioni turistiche* tourist information
l' Inghilterra (f.) England
l' insalata (f.) salad
invece instead
io I
irlandese (m. and f.) Irish
italiano, -a Italian

L

l' the (sing.)
la the (f. sing.)
là there
lascia: mi lascia il suo numero? will you leave me your number?
il latte milk: *al latte* with milk
le the (f. pl.)
le you, to you: *le piace?* do you like it?
la lettera letter
il letto bed: *una camera a due letti* a twin room
libero, -a free
la limonata lemonade
il limone lemon
la linea telephone line: *rimanga in linea* hold the line

la lira lira
il locale a train stopping at all stations
il lunedì Monday

M

la macchina car
la macelleria butcher's shop
il maiale pork
mal: mal di denti toothache; *mal di stomaco* stomachache
la mancia tip
mangiare to eat
il manzo beef
margherita: la pizza margherita pizza with tomato sauce and mozzarella cheese
il marito husband
il martedì Tuesday
matrimoniale a room with a double bed
massimo maximum: *al massimo di* for a maximum of
me me: *per me* for me
il melone melon
meno less
il menù menu
il mercato market; *il supermercato* supermarket
mezzanotte midnight
mezzo half: *mezzo chilo* half a kilo
mezzogiorno midday
mi me, to me: *mi dispiace* I'm sorry; *mi piace* I like; *mi lascia il suo numero?* will you leave me your number?
mila thousand(s)
mille a thousand
minerale mineral
mio my, mine (m. sing.)
misto, -a mixed
molto very

N

il/ la negoziante shopkeeper
niente nothing, no: *niente dolce, grazie* no dessert, thank you
no no
noi we, us
noleggiato hired: *ho noleggiato* I have hired
il nome name
non not
la notte night
il numero number: *il numero undici* (room) number eleven

O

occupato busy: *è occupato* he's busy
oggi today
l' olio (m.) oil (olive): *all'olio* with olive oil
l' ombra shade: *all'ombra* in the shade
oppure or
ora hour, time: *a che ora?* at what time?; *che ore sono* what time is it?
l' orario (m.) timetable, schedule, opening hours
l' ostello (m.) hostel: *l'ostello della gioventù* youth hostel
ottimo excellent

P

il pacchettino airmail parcel: *le faccio un pacchettino?* shall I gift-wrap it?
il pacchetto package, parcel
il panino bread roll
parlare to speak
il parmigiano parmesan cheese
parte it leaves: *a che ora parte?* at what time does it leave?

la partenza departure
il passaporto passport
la pasta pasta, cake
la pasticceria patisserie
la patente driving license
la pensione small hotel: *mezza pensione* half-board; *pensione completa* full board
per for, to: *per cortesia/per favore* please; *per me* for me; *per Vicenza* to Vicenza
permesso excuse me, may I come past/come in?
però but
la persona person
la pesca peach
il pesce fish
il pezzo piece: *un pezzo di formaggio* a piece of cheese
piace: le piace? do you like it?
piacere how do you do?
il piano floor: *il primo piano* first floor
la pianta map
il piatto dish: *piatti* (pl.) *del giorno* dishes of the day
piccante spicy
piccolo, -a small, little
il piombo lead: *senza piombo* lead-free
la piscina swimming pool
più more, plus
la pizza pizza
la pizzeria pizzeria
po': un po' a little, *un po' di . . .* a little (of)
poi then, anything else?
il pollo chicken
il pomeriggio afternoon
il pomodoro tomato: *al pomodoro* with tomato
il pompelmo grapefruit
il portafoglio wallet
porta: ci porta? (will) you bring us?

posso? can, may I?
il posto place, room: *c'è posto?* is there room?
il pranzo lunch, main meal
preferisco I prefer
prego don't mention it, may I help you?
prendo I'll have: *prendono* they'll have
prenotato reserved: *ho prenotato* I have reserved
la prenotazione booking, reservation
il prezzo price
il primo the first: *il primo (piatto)* the first course; *il primo piano* the first floor
la presa di corrente electrical outlet
presento: le presento la mia collega? (may) I introduce my colleague?
la profumeria perfume shop
pronto here is: *pronto/i il caffè* here is the coffee
pronto? hello?
il prosciutto ham
prossimo, -a next
può can he/she/you (polite form): *può firmare?* can you sign?

Q

la quaglia quail
qualcosa something: *qualcosa da bere* something to drink
quale? which one?
qualsiasi any
quando? when?
quanti? how many?
quanto? how much?: *quanto costa?* how much does it cost?; *quant'è?* how much is it?; *quanto viene?* how much does it come to?
quarto: un quarto a quarter: *le due e un quarto* a quarter past two

questo, -a this, this one
qui here
quindi then

R

il raffreddore a cold
la ragazza girl
il ragazzo boy
il rapido fast train
regionale typical of a region
il resto the change
richiamare to call back
ripetere to repeat
il riso rice
il risotto risotto
il ristorante restaurant
il ritardo delay: *in ritardo* late; *sono in ritardo* I'm late
il ritorno return
rosso, -a red
la rosticceria a take-out establishment specializing in roast meats
la roulotte caravan

S

sai: sai dire? can you say?
salato, -a savory, salty
il salmone salmon
la salsa sauce
la salumeria cooked meats shop
scozzese (m. and f.) Scottish
scusi? excuse me?
il secondo (the) second; the second course
la sede the main office, head office
la segretaria secretary

la segreteria telefonica the answering machine
il semaforo the lights
sempre always, still: *sempre dritto* straight ahead
senza without
le seppie (pl.) cuttlefish
la sera evening
il servizio in camera room service: *il servizio sveglia* wake-up service
servono: mi servono i passaporti I need your passports
sì yes
siamo we are
il signor . . . Mr . . .
la signora lady, Mrs . . .
il signore gentleman
la signorina Miss . . . , young lady
singola single
sinistra left: *a sinistra* to the left
soltanto only
sono I am
specialità a typical dish
le stagioni seasons
stamattina this morning
la stanza bedroom
la stazione railway station
la sterlina pound sterling
storico, -a historic
la strada road
subito immediately
il suo his/her/s; your/yours (polite)
il supermercato supermarket
il supplemento supplement

T

il tabaccaio tobacconist
la tavola calda self-service restaurant
il tè tea
tedesco, -a German
il telefono telephone
la televisione television; TV set
temporaneamente temporarily
la tenda tent
la terrazza balcony
il tipo type
il/ la titolare the owner (of the firm)
la toilette toilet
il tonno tuna fish
torna he, she comes back: *quando torna?* when does he come back?
la torta cake, sweet
tra between, within: tra un'ora in an hour's time
la trattoria small family restaurant
troppo too, too much
la trota trout
trovare to find
il turno: chiuso per turno weekly closing day

U

l' ufficio (m.) office: *in ufficio* in the office; *l'ufficio postale* post office
un' a, an (f. sing.)
un a, an (m. sing.)
una a, an (f. sing.)
l' utilitaria small car

V

vada go: *vada dritto* go straight on
la valigeria leather-goods shop
vede you (polite form) see
vegetariano, -a vegetarian
verde green
verdura vegetables
verso at around, toward: *versi le tre* at around 3 o'clock
il viaggio journey trip
il vice-direttore assistant manager
vicino, -a near
il vino wine
il vitello veal
volte: tre volte al giorno three times a day
vorrei I would like
il vostro: il vostro vino della casa your house wine
vuole? would you like?

Z

la zuppa soup
lo zucchero sugar

ENGLISH-ITALIAN

A

a, an un, uno (m.); un', una (f.)
absent as**sen**ti (pl.)
adult l'a**dul**to (m.)
after **do**po
afternoon il pome**ri**ggio
agreed, OK d'ac**cor**do
air conditioning l'**a**ria condizio**nat**a (f.)
airmail parcel il pacchet**ti**no
also **a**nche
always, still s**em**pre; *straight ahead* s**e**mpre dr**i**tto
American ameri**can**o, -a
and e
answering machine la segreter**i** telef**o**nica
any qual**si**asi
anything else? p**oi**?
appetite appe**tit**o; *bon appetit* bu**o**n appe**tit**o
appetizer l'anti**pas**to (m.)
appointment l'appunta**men**to (m.)
to arrange fis**sa**re
arrival l'ar**riv**o (m.)
as far as, to, until **fi**no; *as far as the lights* **fi**no al sem**a**foro; *until two o'clock* **fi**no alle d**u**e
as, like c**o**me; *as a first course* c**o**me pr**i**mo
assistant manager il v**i**ce-dirett**o**re
at, to a
Australian australi**an**o, -a

B

balcony la terr**a**zza
bank la **ban**ca

bar il bar
bath il **ba**gno
beans fagi**o**li
bed il **le**tto; *a twin-bedded room* una c**a**mera a d**u**e l**e**tti
bedroom la c**a**mera, la st**a**nza
beef il m**a**nzo
beer la **bi**rra
between, within tr**a**; *within an hour* tra un'**o**ra
bill il c**o**nto
bottle la bott**i**glia
boy il rag**a**zzo
breakfast la colazi**on**e
bring: (will) you bring us? ci p**o**rta?
British brit**a**nnico, -a
bun la bri**o**che
bus l'**au**tobus (m.)
bus stop la ferm**a**ta
busy occup**a**to; *he's busy* è occup**a**to
but per**ò**
butcher shop la macelle**r**ia
butter il b**u**rro

C

cake la t**o**rta
to call back richiam**a**re
campsite il camp**eg**gio
can: he/she/you can (polite) pu**ò**; *can you sign?* pu**ò** firm**a**re?; *can you say?* (informal) s**a**i d**i**re?; *can, may I?* posso?
Canadian cana**de**se (m. and f.)
car la m**a**cchina; *car rental/lease* l'autono**leg**gio (m.); *small car* l'utilit**a**ria
caravan la roul**o**tte
cashier's counter la **ca**ssa
cathedral il du**o**mo

center il c**en**tro; *city center* il c**en**tro città
certainly c**e**rto
to change cambi**a**re; *can I change. . . ?* **po**sso cambi**a**re. . . ?
change (money) il **r**esto
cheese il form**a**ggio
chicken il p**o**llo
child il bam**bin**o
chop la braci**ol**a
city, town la citt**à**
class la c**la**sse; *first class* p**ri**ma cl**a**sse
closed chi**us**o, -a; *holiday closing* il chi**u**so per f**e**rie; *weekly closing* il chiuso per turno
coffee il caff**è**: *weaker black coffee* il caff**è** l**un**go; *coffee with a dash of milk* il caff**è** macchiato; *small black coffee* l'esp**res**so (m.); *espresso with steamed milk* il cappu**ccin**o
(a) cold il raffredd**o**re
colleague il/la coll**e**ga
commitment l'imp**eg**no (m.)
connection la co**in**cid**e**nza
contract il contr**at**to
cooked **co**tto, -a
cost: it costs **cos**ta
cough drops le g**o**cce
credit card la c**a**rta di c**re**dito
cuttlefish le s**e**ppie (pl.)

D

day il gi**or**no; *per day* al gi**or**no
delicatessen la salumer**i**a
delay il rit**a**rdo; *late* in rit**a**rdo; *I'm late* s**o**no in rit**a**rdo
departure la par**ten**za
dessert il d**o**lce
destination la destinazi**on**e
diarrhea la diarr**e**a

director il dirett**o**re
dish il pi**a**tto; *typical (regional) dish* la specialit**à**; *dishes of the day* I piatti del giorno
document il docu**men**to
dollar il d**o**llaro
don't mention it pr**e**go
to drink b**e**re; *something to drink* qual**cos**a da bere
driving license la pat**e**nte
duck l'**a**nitra (f.)

E

to eat mangi**a**re
employee l'impieg**at**o (m.)
England l'Inghilt**e**rra (f.)
enough **ba**sta; *is that enough? is that all?* **ba**sta così?
evening la s**e**ra
excellent buon**is**simo, -a, **o**ttimo, -a
exchange il c**a**mbio
excuse me sc**u**si
excuse me, may I pass through/come in? perm**e**sso
expensive c**a**ro, -a
express train il r**a**pido

F

fillet il fi**le**tto
to find trov**a**re
(the) first il pr**i**mo; *the first course* il pr**i**mo (pi**a**tto); *the first floor* il pr**i**mo pi**a**no
fish il p**e**sce
flavor il g**u**sto
floor il pi**a**no; *first floor* il pr**i**mo pi**a**no
for, to p**er**; *for me* per me
free l**i**bero, -a
French fran**ce**se (m. and f.)
fried fr**i**tto, -a

from d**a**
fruit la fr**u**tta
fruit vendor il fruttiv**e**ndolo
fully booked al comp**le**to

G

garlic l'**ag**lio (m.)
gas la ben**zin**a
gentleman il sign**o**re
German ted**e**sco, -a
girl la rag**a**zza
glass il bicchi**er**e
to go an**dar**e; *go* (polite) v**a**da; *go straight ahead* v**a**da dr**i**tto; *the way to. . . ?* per an**dar**e a . . . ?
good b**uo**no, -a
goodbye arrive**der**ci
goodnight b**uo**nan**o**tte
grapefruit il pomp**el**mo
Great Britain la Gr**a**n Bret**ag**na
green v**e**rde

H

half m**e**zzo; *a half kilo* un m**e**zzo ch**i**lo
ham il prosci**ut**to; *cured ham* il prosci**ut**to cr**u**do
handbag la bor**set**ta
have: I have ho; *he/she has* h**a**, *you have* (polite), h**a**, *we have* abbi**am**o; *do you have any cheese?* h**a** del form**a**ggio?
hello, good evening b**uo**nas**e**ra
hello, good morning b**uo**ngi**o**rno
hello, hi, bye ci**ao**; *hello (on the phone)* pr**o**nto?
here qu**i**; *here is . . .* **e**cco; *here is the coffee* **e**cco il caff**è**; *here they are* **è**ccoli
historic st**o**rico, -a
holiday le f**e**rie: *holiday closing* chi**u**so per f**e**rie
hostel l'ost**e**llo (m.); *youth hostel* l'ost**e**llo d**e**lla giovent**ù**

hotel l'al**ber**go; *hotel manager* l'albergat**o**re (m.), l'albergatr**i**ce (f.); *small hotel* la pensi**o**ne: *with half-board* m**e**zza pensi**o**ne; *with full board* pensi**o**ne compl**e**ta
hour, time **o**ra: *at what time?* a che **o**ra?; *what time is it?* che **o**re s**o**no
how are you? (polite) c**o**me st**a**?
how do you do? piac**e**re
how many? qu**a**nti?
how much? qu**a**nto?; *how much does it cost?* qu**a**nto c**o**sta?; *how much is it?* qu**a**nt'**è**?; *how much does it come to?* qu**a**nto viene?
(a) hundred grams etto
husband il mar**i**to

I

I **i**o
I am s**o**no
I'll have pr**e**ndo; *they'll have* pr**e**ndono
I'm sorry dispi**a**ce, mi dispi**a**ce
I would like vorr**e**i
information le informazi**o**ni (pl.); *tourist information* le informazi**o**ni turi**s**tiche
ice cream il gel**a**to
immediately s**u**bito
in in
included incl**u**so; *everything included* t**u**tto incl**u**so
instead inv**e**ce
introduce: (may) I introduce my colleague? le pres**e**nto la m**i**a coll**e**ga?
Irish irland**e**se (m. and f.)
Italian itali**a**no, -a

K

key la chi**a**ve
kilo il chilo
kind gentile; *you are very kind* (polite) **è** m**o**lto gent**i**le

L

lead il pi**o**mbo; *lead-free* s**e**nza pi**o**mbo
leather-goods shop la valiger**i**a
leave: it leaves p**a**rte; *at what time does it leave?* a che ora parte?
left sin**i**stra; *to the left* a sin**i**stra
lemon il lim**o**ne
lemonade la limon**a**ta
less m**e**no
letter la **le**ttera
lift l'ascen**sor**e (m.)
lights (traffic) il se**ma**foro; *at the lights* al se**ma**foro
like: I like mi pi**a**ce; *do you like it?* (polite) le pi**a**ce?
like c**o**me
lira la l**i**ra
(a) little po', un po'; *a little of* un po' di . . .
lunch, main meal il pr**a**nzo

M

managing director il dirett**o**re
map la pi**a**nta
market il mercato; *supermarket* il supermercato
marketing director il dirett**o**re delle v**en**dite
matter: it does not matter non im**po**rta
maximum m**a**ssimo; *for a maximum of* al m**a**ssimo di
may I help you (polite)? des**i**dera?
me me; *for me* per me
me, to me mi
meat la c**a**rne
melon il mel**on**e
menu il men**ù**
midday mezzogi**o**rno
midnight mezzan**o**tte
milk il l**a**tte; *with milk* al l**a**tte

Miss, young lady la signorina
mixed misto, -a
Monday il lunedì
more, plus più
(this) morning stamattina
Mr., sir il signor
Mrs., lady la signora
mushrooms funghi

N

name il nome; *what is your name?* (polite) come si chiama?
near vicino, -a
need: I need your passports mi servono i passaporti
next prossimo, -a
night la notte
no no
not non
nothing, no niente; *no dessert, thank you* niente dolce, grazie
now then allora
number il numero; *(room) number eleven* il numero undici; *will you leave me your number?* mi lascia il suo numero?

O

of di
office l'ufficio (m.); *in the office* in ufficio; *post office* l'ufficio postale; *main/head office* la sede
oil (olive) l'olio (m.); *with olive oil* all'olio
one-way (trip) andata
onion la cipolla
only soltanto
open aperto, -a
or oppure
orangeade l'aranciata (f.)
oranges arance

out, outside fuori; *outside the station* fuori della stazione
outlet (electrical) la presa di corrente
oven il forno; *oven-heated* al forno
owner (of a firm) il/la titolare

P

package, parcel il pacchetto
parmesan cheese il parmigiano
passport il passaporto
pasta, cake la pasta
patisserie la pasticceria
peach la pesca
perfume shop la profumeria
person la persona
pharmacy la farmacia
phone card la carta telefonica
piece il pezzoí; *a piece of cheese* un pezzo di formaggio
pizza la pizza; *pizza with tomato sauce and mozzarella cheese* la pizza margherita
pizzeria la pizzeria
place, room il posto; *is there room?* c'è posto?
platform il binario; *from platform (four)* dal binario (quattro)
please per cortesia, per favore; *please go to, please sit down* accomodi, s'accomodi
pork il maiale
postcard la cartolina
pound sterling la sterlina
prefer: I prefer preferisco
price il prezzo

Q

quail la quaglia
(a) quarter quarto; un quarto; *a quarter past two* le due e un quarto

R

railway station la stazione
raw; cured crudo, -a; *cured ham* prosciutto crudo
red rosso, -a
rented noleggiato; *I have rented* ho noleggiato
to repeat ripetere
reservation la prenotazione
reserve: I have reserved ho prenotato
restaurant il ristorante; *small family restaurant* la trattoria
return il ritorno
rice il riso
right destra; *to the right* a destra; *on the right* sulla destra
risotto il risotto
road la strada
roll (bread) il panino
(a) room with a double bed matrimoniale; *a twin-bedded room* una camera a due letti
room service il servizio in camera; *wake-up service* il servizio sveglia
round-trip andata e ritorno

S

salad l'insalata (f.)
salmon il salmone
sauce la salsa
savory, salty salato, -a
schedule/timetable l'orario (m.)
Scottish scozzese (m. and f.)
seasons le stagioni
second course il secondo
secretary la segretaria
self-service restaurant la tavola calda
shade l'ombra; *in the shade* all'ombra
shopkeeper il/la negoziante

shower la d**o**ccia
to sign fir**ma**re; *can you* (polite) *sign?* pu**ò** firm**a**re?
single **s**ingola
small, little **pi**ccolo, -a
smoking or non-smoking? fuma**to**ri o non fuma**to**ri?
something qualc**o**sa; *something to drink* qualc**o**sa da b**e**re
sorry: I'm sorry mi dispi**a**ce
soup la **zu**ppa
to speak par**la**re
spicy picc**a**nte
stamp il francob**o**llo
station (railway) la stazi**o**ne
steak la bist**ec**ca
stomachache mal di st**o**maco
straight ahead dr**i**tto; s**e**mpre dr**i**tto
strawberry la fr**a**gola
string beans i fagio**lin**i
sugar lo z**u**cchero
Sunday dom**e**nica
supermarket il supermerc**a**to
supplement il supplem**e**nto
swimming pool la pisc**i**na

T

take-out establishment specializing in roast meats la rosticcer**i**a
tea il t**è**; *with lemon* al li**mon**e
telephone il tel**e**fono
telephone line la **li**nea; *hold the line* rim**a**nga in **li**nea
telephone token il get**to**ne
television, TV set la televisi**o**ne
temporarily temporaneam**e**nte
tent la t**e**nda
thank you gr**a**zie; *that's all, thanks* **ba**sta, gr**a**zie
then qu**i**ndi
then, anything else? p**o**i?

there là; *there is* c'**è**
this, this one qu**e**sto, -a
(a) thousand **mi**lle
thousand(s) **mi**la
thruway l'autost**ra**da (f.)
Thursday il giovedì
ticket il bigli**e**tto
ticket office la biglietter**i**a
tip la m**an**cia
tobacconist il tabacc**a**io
today **o**ggi
tomato il pomod**o**ro; *with tomato* al pomod**o**ro
tomorrow dom**a**ni; *the day after tomorrow* dopodo**ma**ni
too, too much tr**o**ppo
toothache mal di d**e**nti
toward v**e**rso; *at around three o'clock* v**e**rso le tr**e**
town la citt**à**
trade fair la fi**e**ra
train (express) il r**a**pido; *train stopping at all stations* il loc**a**le
trip il vi**a**ggio
trout la tr**o**ta
Tuesday il martedì
tuna fish il tonno; *with tuna fish sauce* al t**on**no
turn **gi**ri (polite); *turn left* **gi**ri a sin**is**tra
twin-bedded room d**o**ppia, camera **do**ppia
type il t**i**po
typical of a region region**a**le

U

understand: I didn't understand non ho cap**i**to
until **fi**no

V

VAT excluded IVA esc**lu**sa
veal il vit**e**llo

vegetable, salad dish il cont**o**rno
vegetables la verd**u**ra
vegetarian vegetari**a**no, -a
very m**o**lto

W

wallet il portaf**o**glio
water l'**a**cqua (f.); *mineral water* l'**a**cqua mine**ral**e; *sparkling mineral water* l'**a**cqua mine**rale** gas**sa**ta (or friz**zan**te); *regular mineral water* l'**a**cqua mine**ral**e non gas**sa**ta (or natur**al**e)
we, us noi
we are si**a**mo
well b**e**ne; *OK, fine* va b**e**ne; *very well, very good* benissimo
Welsh gall**e**se (m. and f.)
what c**o**sa; *what will you have?* c**o**sa pr**en**dono?
what is (it)? cos'**è**?
when? qu**a**ndo?
where? d**o**ve? *where is?* dov'è?
which one? qu**a**le?
white bi**an**co, -a
who? chi? *who shall I say?* chi d**e**vo **di**re?
wine il v**i**no; *your house wine* il v**o**stro v**i**no d**e**lla c**a**sa
wine shop la can**ti**na
with con
without s**e**nza
would you like? (polite) vuol**e**?

Y

yes sì
yesterday i**e**ri

NOTES

NOTES

NOTES